Stock Market Investing for Beginners

Learn How to Enter the Stock Market! Including the Best Platforms for Trading and Common Mistakes and How to Avoid Them

By

Nathan Real

Table of Contents

Introduction

Have you ever asked yourself, "What is stock?" Do you ever wonder what it feels like in investing your excess cash or savings to the stock market? Have you ever tried to become a shareholder of a company, well-known or not? Have you tried to browse what it would be like when you invested or purchased stocks in a stock market? Do you even know what the basics of stocks are? Well, this would probably help you as a guide in your beginner's journey in the stock market.

Stocks are said to be the shares held by the shareholders, the holder of the stock certificate who has a claim to be a part of the corporation's assets and earnings. History has proven that investing in stocks has been one of the most effective and efficient way for individuals to build wealth and raise their passive income. Investing in stock is complex. Hence, stocks are still misunderstood by some people. There are factors that must be taken into consideration before investing in stocks such as the company where to invest and what type of stocks to buy. Thus, stocks usually have two types: the common stock and the preferred stock. When people talk about stocks, they are generally referring to the common stock. In fact, great majority of sock is issued in this form. It represents a claim on profits (dividends) and confers voting rights. On the other hand, preferred stock usually doesn't come with the voting rights. Also, they are given a guaranteed fixed dividend unlike with the common stocks which give variable dividends that varies along the profits or earnings of the corporation for a period.

Investing is risky. You need to enrich your investment strategy and be tactical in order to maintain your investment and attain your desired goals. Therefore, investing is truly about "working smarter, not harder."

Chapter 1: Entering the Stock Market

One of the most interesting realms of finance is capital exchange. There are hundreds of inventories accessible for trade from across the globe. For both budgets, there are sufficient inventories. There are shares that pay just a few bucks a share, and other high-end stocks valued tens of billions of dollars.

Capital exchange is a huge market in which billions of dollars are exchanged every day. People of all walks of life trade in stocks in terms of improving profit. Some people work for short sales or other options that rely on the dropping value of the stock. Business variety is one of the main strengths, and there is enough for all to be involved in.

Knowing how to navigate the stock market needs a professional and performing well. Only the strongest and most experienced traders would be able to reliably identify products that are most likely to perform at their peak.

This guide would clarify how the equity market operates and how value stocks may be found.

Difference Between Stocks and Options

Trading stocks and options are amongst the best opportunities for investment. Many investment companies offer investors both of those services. What are the dissimilarities between those two opportunities to invest?

In a particular company, the stock is a portion of ownership-how much of anything you own at a particular time. You could own as many stock shares in a firm as you could afford.

An option is not a form of real ownership, but a right to choose and trade a certain investment. You have the right, with an option, to buy or sell a specific stock to a certain value within a given period of time.

Derivative and Intrinsic Values

The intrinsic value of stock refers to the real value of an asset or enterprise. The value is related to how much trust people have in a business and how well that team is growing. Due to news reports or other articles concerning the stock, it may also change in value.

An option is focused on the economic value-a security value at a given time. The value of an option is affected by the stock price, and it simply adjusts to the stock changes.

Long or Short-Term?

There are no specific guidelines about how long an option or stock needs to be kept. Options also have an expiration date. That is, an alternative must be pursued within a specified timeframe. You will specify the exact time limit for the expiry of the contract, authorizing you to perform a transaction or selling at a certain cost at that point. You can hold a running option for as long as you like. Any ideas last an hour. Others may stay for a couple of days or even weeks. Knowing the correct time to pick an alternative is crucial to your plan.

Stocks are special in that as much as you find appropriate, you may keep them. Day traders also sell stocks in the course of a day many times. This is important when contemplating the long-term value-increase ability of a stock. For example, at the beginning of 2014, Home Depot (NYSE: HD) saw its stock traded at about $80.

The stock is worth a little more than $185 in 2018. Day-traders also profit within a day from shifts in a stock's valuation. The same Home Depot inventory could start at $185 on a normal day and then go up to $188, drop to $186, and then down to $188 at the last of the day.

What About Dividend Stocks?

Dividend stocks are securities that pay dividends to shareholders, and the prices of such dividends can differ. If their prices begin to grow and the business stays successful, you'd be more likely to make a return from stocks. Shares of dividends can be valuable as long as you accept their efficiency. You'd need to study how often shares you need to buy if you want to take advantage of a dividend portfolio. You'll later hear about a calculation to use in this guide to decide what you'd have to pay on an inventory to have a dollar in dividend payments; this formula will impact the size of the spot you'd like to purchase.

Who Could Benefit from Day-Trading?

There are several groups of individuals who should have benefited more from day trading:

- Those who want better returns over shorter durations can get more from the day-trading phase. It is independent of whether one is trading in options or stocks.

- Anybody who likes to be the master of their life would enjoy day-trading. You will operate similarly to your own timetable for this while selling at a rate where you are relaxed.

- You don't have to be heavily trained to be a decent day-trader. Getting some experience does benefit, which you can read earlier in this part.

- Day traders will operate on any assets they like. Trading websites promote the discovery of exclusive products and opportunities for them. When combined with prescreening software, making the correct options becomes simpler for the day traders.

- People will be enthusiastic, like day-trading, if they want an interesting job atmosphere. In a day trader's job, there really is a boring moment.

What Problems Persist with Day Trading?

As fun as becoming a day-trader may be, you should be mindful of any issues.

- There's still a chance to lose money on a deal. Those losses may also be largely based on how a product travel. This might be severe if they don't put the correct stop-loss instructions.
- Before you can finally start trading, you will have to buy the necessary supplies. In this chapter, these products are discussed later.
- It may be overwhelming to someone not completely trained or able to tackle any of the involving trades. You have to be able to rapidly conduct transactions. The real chance for a transaction may also be incredibly limited.
- Most day-traders can operate from 9:30 am to 4 pm Eastern Time, mostly during the entire

daily trading day. Any traders could swap far past those hours.

- Making a profit entails difficulty. While you can make different minor trades now and then, once you are willing to purchase bigger positions, it is far simpler for you to earn money.

What Does It Take to be a Great Day Trader?

Anyone might be a successful day trader as long as that individual is very well trained and experienced. To make the best of day trading operations, you must have the necessary skills to:

- Successful buyers understand how to recognize the success of securities and can detect those trends of exchange.

- People will know the history of the company whose inventories they regard. Even the overall profits and other internal considerations inside a company may have a strong effect on a stock market feeling.

- Analysis competencies are important to all traders. Traders ought to be able to recognize certain products and how they're changing.

- The strongest traders would stay centered on the specific stocks into which they plan to buy. People also find it convenient to lose count of the products they have available in the market.

- You will have to properly regulate your feelings. Being upset over any exchange is really simple, not going as far as one would have thought. A brilliant day-trader knows what to expect. An investor may look for what is going into a portfolio when checking for contingency plans to avoid future losses lower than they should be.

What You Need for Trading

You'll hear what you should do to win the investment market all through this tutorial. You'll need to get the necessary tools available for trade purposes to make this effective. There are some items you're going to really need that are built to keep track of the competition while still being able to perform well.

Enough Money for Trades

To get started, a sensible budget for day trading will need to be set. You should determine how much money you are prepared to spend on your trades. More specifically, you ought to consider what you're prepared to sacrifice. There's always a chance all your trades might be duds. You should plan your budget on the assumption you are not actually making a profit. Playing the financial markets is about finding ways to make money in the process without spending too much.

To exchange on the exchange, you'll need a minimum capital of $25,000. This is enough capital to help you make several trades without leverage or spreads being needed. In some trades, you might still be able to use leverage or margins, though that is a purely unnecessary solution.

U.S exchanges and securities Commission or SEC states that, if you plan on trading, you need to have $26,000 or more in equity:

1. Anyone who trades four to five times in 5 business days will need $25,000 in equity or more. The SEC perceives day-trading as a process on the same day on which you purchase and sell things.

2. You will have this volume of money available if your portfolio's day-trades equal at least 6 % of your overall trading operation for the next five business days.

If you can, insert more to your day-trading account than the $26,000 required. A bit of extra money lets you work with a buffer. This ensures some freedom in handling whatever trades you wish to complete in the future.

Sensible Strategies

Build a plan with your trades that you can use. Your plan could be focused on such factors as:

- If you get interested in a transaction
- How to stay out of this deal
- The cumulative danger you are at in every transaction
- An overview of how good stock performs
- As you can learn in this tutorial, your financial strategy can contain several techniques in your trading plans, depending on what you find, depending on your analysis, and common sense in general.

Online Resources

To support you handle your transactions, you may have to use professional online tools. There're numerous trading sites that can help you find available commodities, help you conduct transactions, and others that show all the specifics of how commodities travel. You must be presented with historical details from one of those services.

Even a portfolio screener is important to your progress in investing. It allows you to get product statistics depending on unique requirements. You are actually applying different parameters to the software and only making the best choices.

A Strong Mindset

The most critical thing you require is a strong attitude for day-trading. You need to be emotionally prepared to deal and able to consider what might happen, and be ready to react quickly when anything unforeseen occurs. If it's the price that unexpectedly dipped or an opportunity that arrives at the right moment, you need to know when and how to play the stock market and when to keep out. You will need to develop a mentality based on a plan and sticking with it during the whole investing phase. It is possible to lose sight of what you do while you are trading. You could run across some successful trades you didn't intend to see, and maybe you're not completely equipped to make such trades. Perhaps worse, you may feel like dumping a plan because it doesn't succeed over and over again. Don't shirk the plan. Being stubborn and oblivious is important to help you remain focused.

Proper Education

And if you are not allowed to obtain a trade degree in the industry, you should at least have the necessary experience. It's better to take benefit of an educational curriculum that shows you how to make trades and what's open.

If you read this document, of course, then the chances are that you already grasp the many points about online trading. There are numerous online trading institutions that will provide you with knowledge about how the business operates. Companies such as the Internet Trading School, TradePro School, Market Whisper, Day-Trading Academy, champion's Edge Trading, and several other organizations with their own web programs. These applications can also be used by even folks who understand about trading to clear up any doubt one may have on how to exchange properly. You will use them in this tutorial to learn the techniques you'll be thinking about.

Chapter 2: How to Choose the Right Stock for You?

It's crazy how many stocks there are, and you can find stocks from every part of the world easily in any area. The first approach is to know what securities to invest in. It is important to know how to select a warehouse. There are lots of factors to remember when determining which stocks are right for you. These points are important for evaluating any methods you intend to use to invest.

Choose Field Stocks You Understand

The first tip for locating a stock is to search for stock details in an area you have particular expertise about. Investing in stocks is better because you recognize the demand in which stock is sold, the variables affecting the sector, and the uncertainty the stock of interest may be facing.

As long as Home Depot is concerned, you should be aware that the stock is powered by the building and home renovation sector. You will also recognize that the industry includes rivalry in the U.S. and Canada with Lowe's, True Value, Home Appliances, and several other firms. Investigate the Warehouse at Home and the rivalry. Your market experience will make you feel more secure about the product you are buying.

The National Market

The New York Stock Exchange and NASDAQ comprise the vast majority of the worldwide trading volume. That doesn't suggest you ought to confine yourself to just two platforms. You can transact products from numerous markets across the world as well. These include the Shanghai Stock Exchange, the Japan Stock Exchange, Euronext, and the London Stock Exchange. The economy of one nation may also be drastically different from another. For e.g., there may be a bull market in Canada where the trading of the TMX

Group is located or in Germany where people are trading on the Deutsche Borse. A bear market in India, meanwhile, could trigger India's Bombay Stock Exchange and National Stock Exchange to fall in value. So it's best to stay with stocks based on markets that you're comfortable with. Analysis markets outside of the NYSE or NASDAQ would be appropriate. Just because an American stock is doing well, that doesn't mean every other market in the world will do the same. The economies in the U.S. are simpler to evaluate.

Do You Know the Company?

You ought to study the business you intend to invest in. It contains the following things to know:

- What the company does.
- Where it stands.
- The manufacturing sector.
- Any other business rivals.

- Updates what is being achieved by the company; this involves big news reports.

Take SandRidge Resources, Inc. (NYSE: SD), for example. If you hear about SandRidge? The chances are you will not be acquainted with the business unless you hear about the Oklahoma City natural gas and petroleum sector, even whether you live near the company headquarters.

You may be more conscious of Yum! Products, Inc. (NYSE: YUM). This corporation is an agency running fast-food franchises KFC, Pizza Hut, and Taco Bell. You might have easier access to knowledge on what Yum! The brand is doing since the company itself is so famous all around the world.

You have the luxury of investing in businesses you're not acquainted with, but you can do as much homework as possible on the company and how the business works, and how it has developed through the years. Check the website of that company, and read its financial results. Make sure that you have enough details and don't fail to locate data in a warehouse. Having as much knowledge as possible about a business is critical to your success in the sector.

Review Price Trends

The next thing to remember is how a stock's valuation is rising. And the stock has its own pattern on how it can go up or down over time.

One reason to remember is how, over the years, Sears Holdings (NASDAQ: SHLD) has undergone a downward trend in its portfolio. In 2004, Sears Shares saw a significant boost in its market valuation as the stock rose from $20 to $110 over the span of a year. Soon afterward, in 2006, the price fell to $80. In the late part of 2015, the stock exchanged about $20. Since then, the stock had been falling, and two years later also dropped below the $5 level.

Price patterns may be useful, but you can remember how long such patterns have been taking place and whether any major improvements have occurred. The Sears Holdings case is only one of a variety of instances of how market patterns will change. Only because a stock is dropping in value doesn't mean it will continue to go down. There is a possibility the supply might be going back up. Positive economic reports or stronger market confidence among investors may trigger this to happen.

Work with Moving Averages

A smart way to track market patterns is to take a peek at a stock's moving average. That refers to a set of stock market averages over a prolonged period of time.

You might, for example, set a 14-day moving average to see if a stock's valuation is increasing. That calls for the following:

1. Take from each of the last 14 days the selling price of one volume.

2. Put all 14 of those values, so they come together.

3. Break the number by 14.

4. This shows you the total moving average.

5. Produce as many moveable averages as possible for stretches of 14 days. For, e.g., you might match the moving average for March 1-14 with the average for March 2-15, March 3-16, etc.

By using as many statistical averages as practicable, you will get an understanding of how a stock's valuation varies. Fast-moving averages favor day traders. A combination of short and long-term averages can be used when appropriate. That will offer you an understanding of how the economy and the prices of individual stocks shift. Looking at how a stock might change in a short period of time is crucial to your trading success, particularly if you are attempting to do brief trading as a day trader.

Revenue and Debt Relationship

Revenues and loans are a justification for themselves. Such specifics can be contained in a stock's official SEC records.

Clearly, a company that receives more money would do better work. It will have ample funds to compensate its workers, finance numerous activities, and offset any of the costs or loans. While a company's profits are important, the loans it retains may be crippling. This includes costs to acquire new properties, loans, or handle different workers ' wages. Debts, such as monthly debit fees and interest rates, can be ongoing. They can also be one-time payments for materials that are needed for operating needs. It would be risky to invest in a company that carries a lot of debt. This may be a major challenge stopping an organization from reflecting on its overall development.

Note the debt-revenue difference and how it has evolved over time. A company's financial statements can show what affected those numbers and how they might be predicted to continue to shift.

Compare Stock Performance with Other Related Choices

The next suggestion is to examine if some inventories are performing close to what you choose to invest in. This gives you an understanding of how well a product is doing in the same industry and if it is really different from others.

Let's presume you have looked at Macy's stock (NYSE: M). On a map, you can find that Macy's stock is growing up or down in value without any clear long-term pattern. Look at other companies in the same shopping industry to see if Macy's is a successful company in which to buy. You may be searching for details regarding Kohl's (NYSE: KSS) and that the valuation of Kohl's stock has been slowly increasing. Owing to its success, maybe Kohl's would be a safer stock to invest in.

Check different inventories within the same area. If you would be operating with a retail stock, check out four or five market-oriented products and see which one is growing the most. Check those businesses' histories to see what renders these organizations successful or efficient.

What is Best for Short or Long-Term Needs?

Taking a peek at the patterns certain stocks make. How long have those patterns taken place? Perhaps a stock is decreasing rapidly like Sears, or as the Home Depot, it is unpredictable. An exceptionally unpredictable portfolio will be the best fit for day-trading purposes. The Home Store stock can be worthwhile for day trading since the stock fluctuates in value every day.

Meanwhile, it may be easier to hang on to a stock that has a long-term pattern. Is the stock you are involved in, without facing any opposition, steadily increasing in value? Isn't the stock at risk for some major losses in the future? If so, you may want to save and hang onto the stock for the near future. Realizing the right returns will take months or even years, so it'll certainly be worthwhile.

Signs a Stock is Better for Day-Trading

You don't have to swap any exchange that you do. You may take a few stocks over time that are guaranteed to grow in value and hang on to them for months. Here are a number of things to remember whether a stock might be safer for day trading or at least for keeping just a few days at a time:

A stock with a daily amount of or greater than 1 million.

The stock would be more prone to shift in value while the price is high. In only a few minutes, she might make major changes.

Profit holdings are larger.

When you sell a high valuation product, the chance for a big profit is greater. In a few hours, a stock worth $200 a share might shift its value from $10 to $20. Anything that is only $20 per share might be shifting for just a couple of bucks at a time.

Assets are highly unpredictable.

For day trading, a stock whose value varies from 1 to 5 percent every day is great. A stock with a higher volatility rate may shift its valuation so dramatically; you have to be ready to execute those trades.

You're not too preoccupied with the business history.

While it helps to learn how well a firm works and what it does, you may have just a few minutes or hours in stock at that business. At this stage, you do not really have to do any analysis (you can also do some study).

Signs a Stock Works for Long-Term Investing

Now let's speak at the other end of the spectrum in trade. This listing suggests signals that you can spend months in stock, rather than just a few hours:

Why a business earns profits is simple for you to clarify to others.

You might claim, for example, that you realize that Kohl's or Macy's earns its money by selling branded products and fashions to others. Every company that you appreciate is important and can quickly clarify.

For a corporation to remain operating, it doesn't require any control.

Look at the costs a corporation would have to keep operating. Perhaps a corporation will have to invest a lot of capital in equipment and personnel. In some instances, a business is only purchasing from vendors and exporting certain products. In the situation, figure out what it means for a company to run even why there isn't a lot of money to deal with. Any company which does not need a great deal of control may be easier to trust.

A firm has some type of good or service, providing a distinct advantage.

Macy's has several in-house and foreign distributors selling famous high-end products. Kohl's gives its consumers various incentive schemes. Sears provides garments as well as furniture, and also vehicle repair facilities. All three of these retail entities are distinct, but they all have similar stuff about them, which makes them interesting. These distinct characteristics, more specifically, help a company remain alive and successful.

A stock's pattern is steady and doesn't seem like it will shift soon anywhere.

The most significant indicator of this is how effectively a commodity movement performs over the long run. Look through some moveable averages over the last couple of weeks to see how well a portfolio is doing. For, e.g., you can check a stock price over the past 10 to 15

Fridays. This shows how the valuation of the stock changed over time. Stock could be worth investing in if you think the moving average has been gradually increasing. Something that proceeds to go up is a safe investment.

There are still the right products out there that are easy to work out and grasp while getting completely understood patterns.

Chapter 3: Evaluating an SEC Report

One of the best ways to learn about what stocks to invest in is to look at the official SEC reports that are the issue of different companies. Any public company that has a stock must issue one of these reports annually.

How data of a stock is laid out in an SEC report is one of the best strategies you can use to find good stocks in which to invest. You have to identify a lot of specifics in the report as you look at these data.

Background of a Report

To see why incorporating an SEC report into your trading research efforts is so important, you need to see why such reports exist in the first place. An SEC report is a document that must be sent to the United States Securities and Exchange Commission by a publicly-traded company. These reports were required since 1933, when the Securities Act was passed a few years earlier after the major stock market crash. The American government passed this to ensure transparency and specificity of all financial reports from publicly traded companies. This allows investors to make sensible choices about what to invest in. This would discourage them from making stock purchases that they do not fully understand, a problem that primarily caused the 1929 stock market crash.

By sharing all of its information with the public, a business ensures that fraudulent activities do not occur as likely as they do. Any business in which you may wish to invest should have a proper SEC report. The company report should be detailed, and many documents should be provided to prove the company's worth and operations. Any business which fails to provide sufficient SEC information could be suspicious.

10-K Report

The first part of looking at an SEC report is the 10-K report. This is a basic document that provides a complete summary of the performance of a firm. It is different from the report that a business gives its shareholders in that there are no electoral processes provided by the 10-K report.

This document is vital for understanding the workings of a business. It lets you see how the company operates and its different holdings and details. The information is valuable in its fullness. In fact, the 10-K report is the one thing you should be analyzed when looking at the SEC report above all others. It showcases the basics you need to know to make a worthwhile investment.

Summary of Operations

The first point to look at in the 10-K report relates to the operations summary. Including:

1. Background of the Business

The background of the business provides information about what it is doing. For example, Apple's 10-k report (NASDAQ: AAPL) states that the technology firm focuses on making consumer products such as software, networking items, media players, and more.

2. Strategy for the business

The strategy includes how the enterprise moves forward. In the case of Apple, the strategy devises new products and services within the company's own tech platform. This includes, among other features, working with a wide array of third-party development programs.

3. Latest offerings information

The offers must include the physical as well as the non-physical items a company has. Apple's 10-k report has details of the different products it has to offer, such as the iPhone and iPad. It also reports on services and software programs such as the software for the iOS operating system and iCloud cloud storage. Offered general services. The 10-k report also gives details of what a company offers outside of its products. Apple's 10-k report says it offers an extensive customer service team located in the U.S. along with a couple of other call centers in various parts of the world.

4. Competition points

The 10-k report does not require specific names of any particular competitors. It should still include information on how other parties could be offering certain products or services in the same field. In the report, the information could also be found on what a company is doing to try and make itself competitive or distinct from others.

5. Data on research and development

The section on research and development should include what a company is doing to find new products and make them available. It can include information on how much money a company spends on R&D functions. Apple's 10-k report shows that, in 2013, it spent nearly twice as much on R&D operations as it did in 2011.

6. Licenses, patents, trademarks, and copyrights

Any new applications can be included for those legal markers. This shows how committed a company is to what it offers and how prepared it is for any legal issues that may arise. You could benefit from investing in a firm that takes care of its efforts. Don't expect to be overly detailed in this section. The company has only to list how it acquires legal protection to cover any applications that have been sent out, regardless of whether they have been accepted in full or not.

7. Foreign coverage

The foreign data refers to their operations outside of their country of the base. In its 10-k report, Apple lists outsourcing partners across Asia as well as a couple of other groups around North America and Europe. Apple lists this to let people know the company has a foreign presence for both where it sells items and where it makes its products.

8. Seasonal business

The report on seasonality has details of when a firm is doing much of its business. Apple says a significant portion of its sales occurs during the first quarter of the operation of that business. This is around the Christmas season when Apple is selling a large number of gift products.

In the 10-k report, you can use that point to strategize when you want to invest. In the first quarter of the organization, you would have better success investing in Apple because it is a moment when the firm is rising and flourishing.

Financial Outlook Information

The next part of the 10-k report relates to the financial approaches a company uses. A section that reads "Selected Financial Data" should list the financial data. The information may include the following:

- The net revenue from the operations of the business
- The Big Margin
- Costs for development and research
- Operating Revenue
- The effective tax rate an enterprise works with
- The total value of the assets an enterprise has
- The debt the company holds

How many employees a business has; this could explain part of why expenses may, in some cases, start to rise

Financial information should also include historical points. Take the 10-k report, which was released to the public by Intel (NASDAQ: INTC). This includes information on the company's net revenue from 2007 through 2016. The report shows Intel's revenues in 2016 were nearly $60 billion. That total increased to $52 billion in 2013 from $35 billion in 2009. It is important to get historical information to understand how well a business is developing and how its finances have changed. The financial perspective has to be as thorough as possible to know whether or not something is an appropriate choice for your investment.

Balance Sheet

The balance sheet is the next section of the 10-k Report. This should be listed near the report's section called "Financial Statements and Supplementary Data." The sheet is to contain the following information:

1. The company assets

These can include assets for both the short and long term. Such assets may involve currency, inventory, receivable accounts, and other investments. It should also include any equipment or properties that a business holds.

2. The liabilities of the company

Short-term liabilities are orders that could come to pass right now. Customer advances, payable accounts, and any taxes or interest that an enterprise owes should be included. Long-term bonds are debts. These include debts payable for bonds or any lengthy loans to be paid off. In this information listing, the short and long-term debts should be divided into their own sections.

3. Equity of Shareholders

This refers to the assets, minus the obligations. It's a baseline measure of how healthy a business is. The total focuses on what might be returned to shareholders in the event of liquidation of the company's assets and paying off its debts. A business whose total equity is increasing is always worth investing in, since that company stock has a better chance of adding value.

This section should contain information regarding both the preferred and current stock associated with a company. Preferred stock is for those who receive more dividends and may have more access to certain assets in the company. Common stock includes voting rights for major decisions a company makes. (Note: most of the stocks you'll find on the market are common stocks; preferred stocks are typically offered to business people).

The inclusion of these three points on the balance sheet is crucial. There are a couple of strategies that you can use to help you decide whether to make an investment in a company:

Focus on the assets underway. These are the assets that could be converted to cash.

Looking at the current assets helps you find out why the finances of a business may have changed in recent times and whether there has been a significant influx of sales or contracts.

Is it intangible to non-current assets?

Intangible assets include the overall reputation and goodwill a firm holds. A company such as Intel or Apple may have a considerable amount of goodwill because they have produced various products for many people, and each has a dedicated fan base.

Watch for depreciation, which could interfere with an investment.

Here the depreciation refers to the times when the value of the investment shrinks. In the course of time, physical equipment or goods may depreciate, causing the total value of the assets to fall.

Review how long the debts could last.

Some long-term debts might include loans that could last for ten years or more. Others may sunset after a year, thereby allowing a company more flexibility from an acquisition perspective on what it can do.

Calculate the ratio to debt.

The debt ratio can be used to help you figure out how worthwhile investment is. Take overall debt, divide it by total assets. A business with $15 million in debts, for instance, could have $25 million in assets. In this case, the debt ratio would be 0.6. In other words, assets clearly outweigh the debts.

What if it had reversed those numbers? A company with a debt of $25 million and assets of $15 million would have a debt ratio of 1,666.

An enterprise with a higher debt ratio will certainly be dangerous to consider investing in. This type of business would be in real trouble because it has insufficient assets. You should still look at why so many debts the business has attained just to find out what's going on in the business.

Income Statement

The income statement is a valuable guide to read before determining your financial plan. The statement of income refers to the statistics to represent what a company receives over time.

For at least the last three years of business, the statement should include facts. Anything else of history details helps provide you a better picture of where a company is heading and how any costs have been accumulated over the years.

The declaration of income should contain the following details:

1. Complete Wages

2. The proportion of profits

The distinction is the gross benefit or gross loss of the two points.

1. Operational expenses

These expenditures can include R&D, general operating costs, and other non-recurring expenditures.

To get the net taxable gain or loss, deduct the operational costs from the gross profit.

2. Income from running operations

This gain is what an organization receives between debt and taxation.

3. Tax and insurance payments

Depreciation expenses should be found in this portion or reported on a separate line, at least.

To calculate the net gain, deduct interest and tax from the profits.

Orient the plans on companies that gain adequate money when opposed to the costs they have. Taxes might be higher in value when a company is earning more profits, so that's only a normal evolution of how a company is progressing. Tax expenditures can differ depending on where an organization is organized. This might affect the study since it might be a company in another area of the world where taxes are low or zero. In the beginning, the 10-k filing can inform you whether the company is organized outside of where it is headquartered, so you at least know that tax losses will not be important.

Cash Flow Report

The cash flow report is a cash flow study, a calculation of how much money is being exchanged inside and outside a company. It is a liquidity indicator since it tests how effectively a corporation can hold its activities alive. If a company makes the best decisions to pay off loans, control its inventory, or even its R&D operations, it lets you know.

The cash balance analysis contains more detail on what's going on in a company than an income statement. The concern with a declaration of income is that it just deals with issues relating to the currency. The cash flow report contains any asset and feature in the statement and gives you a clearer understanding of what the assets and role of a company are, in fact. That doesn't suggest you can disregard the income statement; all statements are crucial to know whether or not you can spend. Reporting cash flow may include:

1. The Group's total profits

2. The funds flow from activities

The cash flow relates to the income that has been invested over a period of time or received by the company. This may provide information concerning loan transactions, borrower settlement costs, and so on. A cash balance analysis may provide clear explanations that that is the location where the cash flow is. This may entail rises in payable accounts and reductions in receivable accounts.

Of course, you're going to want to choose an organization with a much greater cash balance. There are occasions where a corporation may have a negative cash balance as more capital flows out of the market.

1. The asset portfolios included

Cash used to sell or acquire valuable properties may be mentioned here. Which may provide descriptions of appliances, computers, chairs, stocks, insurance policies, or something else that is being utilized at a time. A company that invests more in its acquisitions will have lower cash flow, but it still continues to expand. Such new ventures may be used for potential gains and to render things more profitable or otherwise competent inside a company.

Such businesses may expend more spending capital or at least save some of their assets for potential use. This is particularly true of software inventories. Tech businesses also budget large sums of capital for new developments or for whatever potential future demands they expect.

2. Cash earned or charged by support

It may mention the money earned by or charged to creditors and owners. Requires trading of securities or shares. Dividend companies can provide specifics of how they pay out dividends. If need be, certain businesses might buy back their stocks.

This 10-k report segment is critical in that it reflects extensively on how the company could develop. There are several factors that cause the cash flow of a stock to rise directly:

- Sales Extra
- Taking out current long-term distribution arrangements for other firms or organizations
- selling products
- Sell off stocks or other commodities
- Any investment that expanded until it was sold off; these involve some capital the firm has

Cash flow decreases may arise due to a number of problems:

- Employee bonuses ought to be compensated out.
- Gain modern appliances or services.
- Bill for vehicle replacements and servicing.
- Having holders pay dividends.

- Lawsuits or other types of litigation; the damages may be factored into the valuation of legal problems.

- This is only a short rundown of the decreases and increases you may find while looking for an investment.

A few helpful suggestions to consider while reading a cash flow chart are:

Although positive cash flow is often good, when the cash flow comes from activities, it is much better.

When the revenue arrives from sales, it means that the firm is producing adequate profits and that further products or new pieces of machinery are accessible to it. An organization with less than half its cash from sales may be too costly to invest in.

Is One Organization Increased Its Operations?

A company with negative cash flow may be halfway into an expansion project. This means the company is attempting to expand and has to invest money in coping with the growth. See what reduced the surge.

Look at the Loan Duration

Loans may be planned years in advance of being due. A loan can also be paid back earlier. Check if and over what time the debts are being charged.

To understand the meaning of cash flow, take a look at WorldCom's illustration. In the 2000s, the stock of the business dropped apart in a spectacular fashion. Many people saw WorldCom's revenue development was substantial, but they did not pay attention to the cash flow. What the investors didn't realize was that WorldCom's cash balance was very weak and substantially weaker than net profits. WorldCom could not spend and be losing money amid all its rise in sales. Any investor who saw weak cash flow from WorldCom may have made the right step and chose not to invest in the stock directly. Given how WorldCom broke apart, the safest bet must certainly have been to keep away.

Legal Proceedings

An overview of a report's court action is important. This applies to the litigation or other complex legal cases a company is going through. There are cases outside of regular proceedings.

Let's switch back to a 10-k filing from Apple. In their 2013 paper, Apple published details about a few court proceedings it had encountered.

Apple was losing about $370 million in a 2010 lawsuit against a corporation that argued who Apple had infringed those patents. It also covered a 2012 event in which Apple was awarded over $1 billion by another action.

The segment on legal action should provide information on the official identities of the court cases concerned and how much money they were worth irrespective of whether the judge favored. Even detail should be given about whether the action was launched.

You may want to look for more details on every company's court actions by investigating the cases on the organizations' pages that handled such cases. For example, a lawsuit considered by the Department of Justice in the United States may be investigated electronically at www.justice.gov. You will need to go and www.uscourts.gov to provide more details about lawsuits being conducted within those U.S. jurisdictions. These pages will provide you with comprehensive details on legal hearings and additional material specific to certain events.

In this section of a 10-k filing, a corporation can be clear and transparent on the legal proceedings. An organization that is able to provide as much detail as possible regarding these cases is much easier to trust, and the business is not reluctant to discuss any of its issues. You can still glance at such unofficial pages when a corporation may also want to withhold details regarding its legal problems.

Risk Factors

The 10-k study describes the risk factors a company faces. These considerations provide worries a company thinks would have a significant effect on its potential earnings. Think of it as SWOT analysis' W component.

The 10-k report by Intel mentions various risk factors that could harm the company. The study shows how the organization is having trouble forecasting demand for its goods. It also addresses how Intel experiences substantial rivalry and is therefore exposed to several factors in overseas markets that may potentially create a difference in how much the organization is capable of earning sales and maintaining itself operating.

The threats mentioned here can involve both the global sector and business-related concerns. Intel reports that it is a danger of product flaws or failures that may harm its goods. This risk could result in recalls or major costs, not to mention the possibility of undermining Intel's credibility.

Both of these points on the 10-k report are important for you to evaluate while determining which stocks to invest in. Review the whole report before conducting a transaction so you can appreciate where a company is heading and how it might actually affect its valuation.

10-Q Report

A 10-q filing parallels a 10-k filing that reports on a company's quarterly job.

Let's look at a 10-q filing, published in July 2017 by the Coca-Cola Corporation (NYSE: KO). This was from April until June 2017, with financial details across the year.

The 10-q study by Coca-Cola comprised a variety of important things:

1. Financial statements related to corporate income, operating expenditure, taxation, and varying expenditures

Many of the financial aspects outlined in the 10-q filing are similar to what is included in a 10-k study. This also offers a clearer understanding of what a business just did.

2. Information about any major changes that occurred during the previous quarter

In its 10-q filing, Coca-Cola reported that it had acquired a plant-based beverage firm and also franchised some of its operations in China.

3. Agreements signed with some parties

At a specified period, these arrangements can be transactions between particular individuals for services and goods from separate companies and offers.

4. Lawsuits and risk factors pending

In certain instances, you would refer back to an organization published in the last 10-k report. This is about situations where the consumer has not had something new happen.

You should also provide information to some court proceedings which are currently pending.

8-k Report

The Latest Filing is also regarded as the 8-k audit. Companies discuss this because they have significant activities they wish to let the public know about. The research is also on something that allows a business to rise in scale. In some situations, the research is on certain daunting topics that may be warning flags about the investing plan. An 8-k filing for consideration of any of the following may be filed:

- Issuing Insolvency
- Entering or rejecting a binding content deal

- Completion of a big takeover bid
- Any incidents that trigger an adjustment to a financial commitment
- Cases where forecasts that a company is supposed to receive are drastically adjusted in value; this typically occurs when something's quality declines
- Changes to ethical business policy
- The presentation of core problems and inventions to be placed to the ballot of shareholders

The 8-k Coca-Cola Business study published in mid-February 2018 is one indication of that. The firm released an 8-k filing claiming that the organization had an excellent financial performance for the fourth quarter of the previous fiscal year. The study contained detail about many of the financial changes happening at the moment. In December 2017, Coca-Cola submitted an 8-k filing reporting a resignation of a key member of the business management. In October 2017, another research from the same firm claimed the business had a positive performance in the third quarter.

There are no restrictions on how many 8-k files a company may put out. You'd have to glance at how it mentions these. When writing these reports, an organization can be very comprehensive and straightforward so customers can consider what leads a business to move in any manner.

Internal Functions

SEC reports may provide descriptions of all the internal operations that an organization requires. It provides a thorough overview of how the company is run and who is in charge, as well as any unusual acts that certain persons participate in. There are three basic records to analyze when examining an enterprise's organizational operations.

Proxy Statement

The proxy statement applies to details from management and the company's reports. It must be submitted before an annual meeting where shareholders are permitted to vote on operations taking place within the organization. The study gives you an overview of how the company administration functions and how the people concerned could get compensated. It also mentions potential questions about conflicts of interest that individuals might have with such auditors.

To grasp the workings of a proxy document, let's look at the document issued in April 2017 by Southwest Airlines (NYSE: LUV). The declaration contained the following points:

- Details about how citizens should become interested in voting
- How democratic procedures work
- The specifics of the persons concerned and any conflicts of interest they might have

The Southwest Airlines proxy statement stated that owing to numerous reasons linked to expertise and abilities, separate Board members could continue to retain their seats. -- individual was identified citing their experience in education, prior employment in the aviation sector, and so on.

Details Regarding How to Pay Employees

Southwest listed unique incentive details that executives will be entitled to receive depending on those success criteria. This provides the volume of revenue handled at a specified period. Performance rewards and promotions can be laid out in a proxy document. Requires future payments, as well as other incentives such as private car use or unique travel facilities.

Functions Report

The classification of who is on the audit committee has been listed to describe how the auditing method will be structured inside the company.

You will locate corporation proxy documents by doing the following:

1. Go to the SEC website and check the report on EDGAR.

2. Join the individual company that you want details for.

3. Scan for a report that is titled DEF 14A. This gets its name as the final proxy statement, according to Section 14(a) of the Stock Exchange Act.

What is interesting about the proxy statement? The proxy statement is essential for a company to notify shareholders regarding the corporate executive functions. It helps us realize that a company has a reasonable strategy in motion to affect the path the company would take in the future as those decisions are to be taken.

You should suggest participating in firms that have open and clear proxy records. Sometimes those companies are easy to trust, and they want customers to grasp their operation's workings.

Schedule 13D

Schedule 13D is a part of SEC filings, covering details about who owns shares. A firm must file it within ten days of a person acquiring 5 percent or more of any security. This provides information on how much of the company's shares might be managed by one person. It could be a sign that one person could have a heavy influence on a business. The Report on Schedule 13D must include:

- Details on safety
- Information about the person who was securitized
- That should include the contact information and background of a person. Any such person's criminal records should be listed, as appropriate.
- The financing source for the transaction

- The money occasionally comes from leveraged or borrowed funds. A transaction that uses money is always better when the investor actually has complete control.

- The reason someone acquires these shares; it's also called the transaction purpose

- This could be because an investor is very much interested in a particular company and feels the stock is undervalued. It could also be a sign that someone is trying to acquire a significant portion of the company. Even those who try to get involved in a hostile takeover should be listed here.

- Any contracts or relationships within the business which the investor has with other people

- Letters and other documents telling how the transaction took place

The form in Schedule 13D is part of the SEC filing that should be reviewed for details and to determine whether someone wants to acquire a significant number of shares.

Form 144

Form 144 deals with how the stocks are made publicly available. Form 144 must be filed when the company plans to sell stock to someone associated with it. This includes an executive, a director, or another figure.

Form 144 is a two-page document that is simple. It has the following details to be filled out:

- Name of the Stock issuer
- Title of the securities class which will be sold
- The number of shares to go on sale
- The market value of said shares
- How much stock is outstanding?

- When expected to sell the shares

The names of the securities exchanges used at a given time Information about any other securities that the person selling the shares has sold in the last three months

Form 144 should be a factor in your investment strategy as you look at how the shares are made publicly available. Sometimes a report on Form 144 is a sign that someone in a company wants to retire and will sell off their shares. In other cases, it could be a sign that something big will happen in the business, like someone else buying out part of that entity.

Added Tips

Anything that goes into the SEC reports of a company will give you a good idea of how a business is run and what makes it exceptional or distinct. While the listed information is worthwhile, there are many intricate parts of an SEC report that you should also delve into. These features tell you more about the stock and can help you formulate your investment strategies.

Review the EPS

Seeking the EPS is a valuable strategy to use. This refers to one stock's earnings per share. Although a company does not have to declare that total in its SEC report, you can still easily figure this out:

1. Look up the net income shown in the report.

2. Divide that net revenue by the number of shares held by the investors.

3. That should give you an idea of how much money each share is involved in.

This is a good measure of how well an enterprise is doing. When the EPS is high, that means the business grows and evolves. This might be a good time to invest, but you should still look into why the total is moving up as much as it is. Sometimes the EPS may be increasing because some of its shares were bought back from others by the business. Also, the EPS could go down because more shares were issued by the business. Whatever the case may be, you must determine how the EPS is formed and why that total is where it is situated.

Don't Forget Assumptions

An EPS could include a series of company assumptions that produce the document. These are based on past earnings, total forecasts, and general business plans as time progresses. Decide how realistic those hypotheses are. A business with a small growth rate of 1 to 2 percent could say it has expectations of 3 to 5 percent growth. This is sensible because it shows the company is growing and becoming more visible. However, as it seems unrealistic, a business that claims it will experience an extremely high increase, such as from 2 percent to 15 percent growth, should be avoided. Any business that doesn't make assumptions couldn't think about the future. It might take for granted that certain functions will remain sluggish or, in some way, lacking.

Consider Economic Conditions

Consider the overall economic conditions of the undertaking in question as you review the SEC report. Sometimes that could involve the economy as a whole. In other cases, it only involves a smaller economic segment. Consider how the economy evolves or not.

A company's net income or near earnings should be compared with the sales revenue it receives. More importantly, it should be analyzed in relation to what the business environment might be like at a given time. The business climate is sometimes healthy, or it might be that a business has difficulty growing and developing.

Conditions within a region in which a company operates could also be a factor. One part of the world could be a focus for an international organization. Yum! Brands, for example, are focused on the United States, Canada, the United Kingdom, and China. These four markets have their own single economic climate. Examining the international factors surrounding a stock gives you an idea of how some regions help or hinder a business. The gains a company has in China could, for example, offset the losses in the US.

Watch for One-Time Changes

Looking at the details of an SEC report, look carefully at some individual one-time changes that might occur as they could have a direct impact on your investment.

There are many reasons why an enormous one-time change could appear on a report:

• An enterprise could have invested in some new equipment or inventory. These include totally new things a company has never had any use for before. This could indicate a company attempting to expand.

• It may also recommend that there is a lawsuit or other legal action that an undertaking has just experienced, which could have resulted in a substantial amount of money paid out as a result of a court fight.

• The reason for the change could be an acquisition of another company.

Watch For Confusing or Vague Content

Another aspect to note when reviewing SEC reports is that there are many confusing SEC reports that could be. They could contain lots of terms you don't know about. Perhaps the reports include vague documents, or certain bits of information are not listed, even though the SEC states that they should be listed. This is often a sign that something a company is trying to hide.

What If a New Version of a Report Is Issued?

A business might sometimes issue a new version of an SEC report. The most common reason this happens is the inaccurate accounting practices a business has engaged in. Perhaps a company may have participated in false accounting by knowingly misleading about the revenues.

Any company which issues an SEC report revision may not be trustworthy. Look for details about why you updated the report before contemplating purchasing the product.

What About the Chairman's Letter?

The letter from the chairman is a text in a report from the SEC, which most people overlook. It is basically a report to customers as to what a company is doing and how it is doing.

The letter has a lot more to it than you would expect. Reviewing a letter from the Manager is one of the strongest techniques you might use to uncover the way an organization is going. It all comes from the chief of first-hand market experience. The Chairman should state when reading the letter:

- Inside the company, the financial strengths and problems are focused on leverage, cash flow, and other factors.

- The difficulties which the organization faces. These involve problems relevant to rivalry, industry concerns, or even the environment at large.
- Current steps are conducted to render the company financially more competitive, regardless of whether they require growth or cost-cutting acts.
- The continuity of the approach of the company, even how the method being employed, varies significantly from what it was a few years ago.
- Detailed and simple to understand the post. The Manager, after all, is the one whose career may be on the line based on how well a company does.

SEC files can be difficult to find because they can be complex and comprehensive. The more you study what's in an SEC report, the better it would be for you to determine the business you should take advantage of by investing.

Chapter 4: Understanding the True Value of Stock

You might have a strategy to find cheaper stocks while you are looking for stocks on the market. But thinking about various underlying factors in stock is even more important. Sometimes the value of a stock isn't as big as the official total says it is. That is, it overvalues stock.

At the same time, a firm is doing very well, but this is not reflected in the stock price. Would you like to buy a stock for $150 per share only to find out later that there was at the same time another stock with a better prospectus available at $30? If you knew what she had to offer at the time, you would probably prefer to take the latter.

You will need to look at several points relating to how well a stock performs so that you can make the most of an investment. This chapter deals with some strategies to use to determine if a stock is overvalued or undervalued.

P/E Ratio

A useful strategy to use when reviewing the value of stock really is to understand the P / E ratio. That is the ratio of price-earnings. This measurement demonstrates what investors will spend on stock. Investors will expect to get more earnings overtime when the total is higher. The stock is considered undervalued if the sum is poor. That means the stock is trading below what the perceived value could be. It could make buying an interesting product, thanks to how at this juncture it is considered a minor bargain. The P / E ratio measurement for obtaining:

1. Take in stock market price.

2. Earnings split by half. The EPS is the net income divided by the shares outstanding.

3. That gives you the ratio P / E.

The total value of the P / E ratio refers to the value that the stock market holds on that product. The investment market likes this better because the amount is larger. That is, the stock is something that consumers would like to purchase.

Here is an example of how the P / E ratio functions. Heading back to Macy's, you could see the stock priced at $26.26. The EPS is now at 2.28. This is focused on the $697 million net profits being split by the 304.57 million outstanding stock Macy's owns. By dividing the value of the stock and the EPS, we get a total of 11.52.

What does this example mean, then? It suggests an investor would be willing to pay $11.52 for each dollar of current Macy earnings. This is an inexpensive sum, since it means consumers would not pay that much on the stock to buy. The low P / E ratio indicates that if you are looking to buy anything a little cheaper on the market, Macy's stock may be worth investing in.

What If a Company Is Losing Money?

When you look at the P / E ratio, a company that is losing money will have an N / A mark on its stock report. Although you could technically calculate a negative ratio to show that a firm is losing money, it's easier to use the N / A listing as an indicator that people don't necessarily expect to gain much from the stock based on their earnings. That may be a sign of too risky a stock. It could also be a sign that a business may have undergone some expansion plan or legal issue, which could cause it to lose money temporarily.

In any situation, the only thing to do is figure out if a corporation is losing revenue. Look into the company's previous results to see what could have been the P / E ratio during better periods. Sometimes the P / E ratio could only dip briefly as a business grows and will rebound back to its original value once those efforts have been completed.

The Optimal P/E Ratio

Image of the Macy indicates the business is earning profits and not failing. Is an 11 percent P / E ratio good? There are no clear solutions as to whether a stock has the strongest P / E ratio. If you are trying to find decent value, you can look for stocks with low overall P / E. A stock that trades its earnings a few times can be cheaper than something that trades 12 times its value or more.

Consider several stock P / E ratios within the same sector. Stock in the technology sector with a P / E ratio of 25 may be interesting, but another stock in the same industry with a ratio of 14 maybe even more attractive.

Watch for Inflation

When looking at the P / E ratio, be aware of what the inflation rate is. Typically, this measurement is lower when the rate of inflation is high. This is because a firm's earnings may be skewed somewhat. As the dollar's power increases, it will seem as if a company is making more money. That rise is due to more dollars being factored into transactions. The cost of replacing assets is on the rise, just like the prices of other market staples.

Consider how the rate of inflation has changed over time as you look at a stock's historical data. Did you notice cases where the P / E ratio has dramatically shifted? That could be due to the rapidly changing inflation rate.

Inflation just takes a couple of months to make a difference. The inflation rate in the US was at 0 percent in May 2015. That total went to 1 percent in February 2016. In November 2016, it would become 2.1 percent. It takes a few months to make a sizable change to the inflation rate, but that shift will be noticeable when you look at investments.

Price/Earnings Growth Ratio

The next metric to remember while analyzing a stock's real valuation is the price/earnings growth ratio. This is an indicator of whether a stock is underpriced or whether the valuation added to it is strong. It could mean the stock is an incredible bargain based on the findings you find.

It is a calculation that can be measured using the following equation:

1. Calculate stock ratio P / E.

2. Divide this by the increase in average earnings per share.

Say a corporation with a share price of $ 50. Last year's EPS for that business may have been $4. The amount may have been as big as $6 this year. Then you measure the P / E ratio by dividing 50 by 6 to hit 8.33. Now split the earnings by taking six separated by four separated by 1. That'd earn you a 0.5. This is calculated as a percentage point, which is 50%- earnings per share rise is 50%. Dividing 8.33 by 50 is tantamount to 0.166 PEG.

The PEG in this sample can sound marginal, but when combined with how the market is rising, the business market is selling at a drastic discount. Hence customers pay less for a company's stock that is beginning to expand. With time, the valuation may be higher attributed to the business proving to be more secure.

The PEG offers you an indication of what to expect from a stock you may have kept for a while. It demonstrates the upward trajectory that a stock may be in. I would recommend you stay a bit longer on a stock with a good Board. Even you should store the stock as a preference for day trading as you can check the stock many times a day to create multiple additional trades.

Use Historical Data

The easiest approach to operate with the PEG is to make the most of historical evidence. The illustration listed reflects on improvements in a stock's valuation over the past year. While this read-out will be helpful, to have a better understanding of how it is changing, you may need to dig at more historical details regarding the PEG.

You may, for example, measure the PEG as it was in 2013. You can calculate earnings per share growth from 2012 to 2013 and see if, from the latest data, this correlates with stock. After that, you will use the same formula just to see how the PEG is adjusting with the development from 2015 to 2016 for the stock value from the latter year.

A stock of that PEG is one that is beginning to purchase more customers. With stock rising and industry growing, consumers are becoming more conscious of what's available. They are going to start investing in the specific stock.

Price/Sales Ratio

The next technique to consider is to look at the ratio of price/sales, commonly known as the PSR. It reflects the valuation of the assets of a business as opposed to profits. A stock of a firm that has strong sales suggests that the business is profitable.

The Price / Sales ratio can be measured by doing the following:

1. Find the complete amount of securities outstanding.

2. For any of the last twelve months, add the cumulative revenue.

3. Divide the number of securities in those transaction figures.

4. Divide the current share value by phase 3 performance.

5. This shows you the Trading PSR based on the last twelve months.

You may also swap the cumulative revenue over the past twelve months with the revenues for the new fiscal year, if you wish. It would offer you a more direct response, even though the total may not be that great. Numbers may be used as a guide for the next fiscal year. The assessment over the last twelve months is more objective and reflects on what the market has improved.

If the PSR is low, this means a stock is inexpensive. Compared to the profits that the business receives, it has a minimal expense. Therefore, it is always advised to get in when the PSR is poor as a purchase.

The worst aspect of the PSR is that it's all sales-based. It is tougher for a company to update its revenue figures than changing the forecasts that an accounting committee could make.

Many revenue figures are steady and operate through periods that vary throughout the year. You may foresee how the PSR adjusts based on how an organization does in the sales department and whether the actual profits are projected to improve or not. This provides a simple element of consistency in determining whether to invest in a corporation or not.

Review Many Businesses in the Same Sector

The easiest approach to operate with the PSR is to audit as many companies as possible within a market. This might provide you a tentative insight into what could be a standard PSR in that area. This may entail, for example, calculating three or four inventories in the software industry. A low-ratio company may have an undervalued stock as opposed to the global industry. That is, the money is free. Which is high in value can, therefore, be more costly than required. Major variations may also mean that different firms have their own objectives or intentions to expand or run.

Analyze the Book Value

Another technique to consider when evaluating a stock's real worth is to take a deeper glance at the stock's book value. This applies to the valuation of the properties kept in a portfolio less than the liabilities plus any intangible assets owned by the firm.

The book value corresponds to the inventory kept by an entity on a balance sheet. It determines what the company's owners will get in case the corporation was liquidated. That's a guess, but it's worth investigating. The most significant argument about the book valuation is that it determines how a company operates. An organization with a higher book value could be one that has ample reserves to hold it running.

The Main Concern

There are concerns about how every time the book value does not function. A fast-growing company may have a misleading book valuation as the business continues to acquire more money and attempts to make any practical improvements about how it runs. Businesses with fewer physical assets may pose a challenge. A bank portfolio may have a high book value, for instance, since that bank has many physical branches and ATMs. An online bank stock is distinctive in that the online banker has no other branches and does not have much to no advertised ATMs. As for every other metric, you need to know what the book prices are for different firms in the same market. Think of what makes a company invest too much in its inventory, only to maintain and work its general activities.

Even the intangible assets that an organization has could be a concern. Perhaps because of a legal dispute or a scandal involving a particular product or service, the credibility of a company has been destroyed. While it could restore credibility over time, it might put a dent in stock. It is not simple to get an exact estimate of the overall effect that such a problem might have on stock.

Evaluate how a company performs when analyzing its revenue, earnings growth, and book value, among other points, while looking at stock prices. There's a good possibility a stock might be a great offer than what you thought it would be.

Chapter 5: Working with Great Trading Platforms

If you don't have a good trading network to deal with, any scheme that you devise for your savings would be useless. A trading site is a software you'll be performing the trades directly. Either of such sites should be accessible via a broker or a financial organization.

For a day trader, the trading platform is a must. The trading mechanism is a normal progression. It used to be that transactions between specific traders or other parties will have to be done in person. There has been the usage of interactive channels since at least the 1970s. The earliest interactive channels will enable users to find current market price statistics, thus encouraging them to submit signals saying they want to do business. The high-speed online environment has developed such that exchanges can accommodate trades at once. People get access to pricing in real-time. What you need is a link to the internet.

Analytics Points

A trading platform should offer you different metrics that can help you distinguish stock choices. Whilst with software, you can find quotations and maps in real-time, you need to be mindful of several other items.

News Feeds Are Vital

A Forum for Trading may have news feeds. This involves stories from various news agencies, including Associated Press and Reuters. The news feeds can send you details on everything that's going on in the business. A platform can also scan for unique stock details using a stream.

A quest for news feeds is one easy process:

1. Check out the stock in which you intend to buy.

2. Check on the stock market and the emblem that it uses.

3. Join the contents by mentioning them as Exchange abbreviations: Symbol. For e.g., if you decided to find details about Cedar Fair Amusements, you might need to enter "NYSE: FUN" in the quest. This lets the software realize that you are searching for the stock of the Cedar Fair described under the symbol Pleasant in the NYSE.

4. Find out the outcome. The results may provide prediction information, SEC reports, and many more. It might also contain some pending incidents.

Try seeking news that's as recent as practicable. You will still use older stock records and get a sense of when a stock has shifted. Anything fresh is often instant and will have a significant influence on the valuation of your stock.

Proper Security Is Needed

The software you are utilizing must be safe, such that your financial information is not compromised or robbed. It needs a secure authentication scheme to enter a username and password to validate your identity.

Encryption is often a must to step through a network. This involves decoding transfers that you are doing so that outside powers cannot hack through a link and understand what you are doing.

Even a format can be used to document all completed transactions. The specification may provide specifics of where a transaction is made, how long it has been for, and so on. Such a requirement helps you to maintain notes so you can prove that, over time, you have made clear transactions.

Support for backups can often be offered on a website, which provides provision for backup servers in situations when the main one may be disabled. It could provide copies of all the details being exchanged, in specific knowledge on the records of both. All those reserves should be subject to the same protection as the primary material.

Financial Points

In a trading network, such additional financial costs may be listed. Ses concentrate on what to invest in finishing deals, or even using a platform:

About how much each exchange would pay, each network has its own price. You should only pay a couple of dollars for each exchange. There may be a fixed rate on a specific deal or a charge, depending on how many securities you purchase or sell. Often because you have more stock, the payments are higher per unit since this is called a bulk sale.

Trades of options include a surcharge on contracts. The additional payment per contract may be nominal in value with an option. It may be inferior to a dollar.

One minimum account can be mentioned. Before you start trading, a lender may ask you to have a certain sum of money in your account. This means you're open to platform trading. Before you start trading, you may need to get $1,000 or more moved to an account with that site. In compliance with SEC requirements, you will require the $25,000 or more in your day-trading portfolio. Any sites may be running exclusive deals. An offer with a qualified deposit could be a guaranteed cash bonus. If you deposit $1,000 or more into an account, for example, you might get $100 in extra money for trading.

Each platform has special margin rates of its own. The margin rates offered for options could fall within a few percentage points of a stock's current value. The standards which a platform uses may vary depending on how long the stock option will be open.

Can This Work In Lieu of a Stock Screener?

If you have a screener to work with, the details from a Trading Platform will be more effective. A dedicated stock-screener account would make it easier for you to find the specific stocks you like. A trading platform won't help you show inventories. Some platforms do offer extensive features for research. They could include their own trigger points and dimensions, allow warnings not to include. You'd have to look for information about how each platform works and what analysis they're offering, and how they can function with you. But a screener is much more detailed and offers you a more comprehensive insight into how you could spend your money and what you can anticipate while making a sale.

What Are the Best Trading Platforms?

Trading platforms have many choices. Investigate as many of these options as possible so that you know what might be suitable and worthwhile for you. Some of the trading platforms are backed by big brokerage houses.

Ally Invest

Ally Invest is a trading platform that lists complete charts of how well stocks move. The platform originates from the popular provider of online banking services. Using this cost $4.95 per trade and does not require any minimum account. Ally Invest also doesn't work with commission-free ETFs or mutual funds. Such investments could cost you extra to buy over the platform. You can also get discounts through Ally Invest. If you're making at least 30 trades in a quarter, you could spend $3.95 each. A day-trader shouldn't have difficulty reaching that threshold.

This solution reveals points that are worthwhile but also frustrating for online banking and financial services. Thanks to a lack of physical branches for its operations, Ally can charge its customers less for services. To some people who want direct contact with a broker, not having physical sites could be a problem.

TD Ameritrade

TD Ameritrade offers a more robust and comprehensive approach to providing inventory information. It features free research tools to help you identify stock patterns and signals. Also valuable is TD Ameritrade's extensive streaming news support, as it provides information from Zacks, Dow Jones, Credit Suisse, and many others. That does cost $6.95 per trade, a little extra to use. When you open an account here, you could get a few hundred dollars extra in a cash bonus, but the bonus will vary depending on the size of the account you have. Also, TD Ameritrade has different trading centers and locations throughout the United States. If you have a need for trading support, you could visit one of these places. You can also access the various branches of TD in Canada through its subsidiary of TD Canada Trust.

Trade Station

Trade Station is famous for providing a comprehensive and detailed trading platform. Recently, the group became popular as it lowered its original minimum total account from $5,000 to

$500, allowing more people to enter the platform. (That doesn't mean you should only have $500 in your account because day traders need more money to fill their positions.) The cost of stock trading may vary depending on the investment. While a flat rate of $5 is available, you could also choose a price point per share based on the volume of trading on the stock. This would involve spending commercially up to $0.01 per share. To qualify for this deal, you'd have to spend at least $1 on the trade; it's clearly a deal designed for people looking to make bigger transactions on the platform.

Over a hundred indicators can be used to work on the platform. Using a stock screener, you can create your own individual indicators based on certain parameters you want to work with, though that might not be as many as what you would get.

Interactive Brokers

Interactive Brokers offers a trading platform that costs $0.005 per share to use and has a minimum account of $10,000. This is intended with a view of frequent trading. It provides a good assortment of investment options and lower margin rates. It does, however, charge inactivity fees for those who do not frequently speak trad. Interactive Brokers also don't offer many educational services for prospective traders. The system is clearly geared towards experienced traders.

Charles Schwab

Charles Schwab was one of the most trusted investment brokerage firms in the US. The organization, which has been in operation since 1971, has hundreds of branches in the United States. For people who need commission-free ETFs and index funds, the firm has its own electronic trading platform for day-trading. The group has Morningstar, Market Edge, and many other popular firms as research resources. The platform lays out stock specifics. Charles Schwab charges $4.95 per trade and demands a minimum of $1,000 from your account. It does not charge any fees for the inactivity.

EOption

EOption could benefit those who are looking for a base platform. There are not many fancy features to this. It only displays a base chart for each stock. It doesn't give you many research options, though that information will be provided by a stock screener. EOption fees $3 per trade, with a minimum account of $500. This platform is best suited for experienced traders with stock screeners that can work as opposed to the research features other platforms offer.

This trading platform information proves they're all varied but can be worthwhile. Make sure that you have the right materials ready to access one of those platforms to start trading.

Don't Forget Simulators

Trading platforms often include simulators to help you acknowledge how the market functions. These simulators focus on education: how to read a layout of a chart, how to execute a trade, and so on. Working with a simulator as close as possible to the actual platform is a necessity so that you know what to do before you actually do business. Check to see if a simulator is available on the platform you choose. Simulator training can make a world of difference. A program like this will help you identify a lot of factors related to how stocks change in value and how patterns can be identified.

Chapter 6: Identifying Patterns in a Stock

Some of the most popular stock market strategies are geared towards patterns. These are instances where, at a given time, something could change within a stock. Patterns show how a stock's price moves while giving signals suggesting something is going to happen. There are many patterns, and when you look at how a stock is evolving, it's easy to figure them out. You can use these to plan your strategies on how you enter or exit trades or when you figure out what kinds of trades you should be doing.

Note: All patterns are identifiable by looking at a traditional stock price chart based on candlesticks. This would show you how something's value moves up and down consistently within a short timeframe.

Reversal or Continuation?

The most important thing about those patterns to notice is that they come in two ways:

1. Reversal - A reversal is where a trend had ended before a pattern started. The stock may have gone up before the pattern, but thereafter the stock will go down.

2. Continuation - A continuation shows that the change in stock prices will continue to move even after the pattern is complete. The pattern could be a brief occurrence, but thereafter the stock will continue unabated.

You can use these points to determine how you should trade in a stock. You may consider buying a stock for later sale, or you may be able to place a call or a put option depending on how the stock moves. Either way, you can always invest in a stock irrespective of whether its value is moving up or down. An interesting thing about continuations and reversals is that they can go on for a long time. It's hard to figure out how long one of those events will be, but you can be sure that something will more than likely happen after a while when a pattern occurs.

Pennant

The Pennant is the first pattern to be observed when a stock is found. It's a continuation pattern showing how the stock will continue to grow in value. At this point, the stock seems to struggle to move up or down in value, but after a while, the stock will break out of the pennant and continue to move towards the same position it was in at the beginning.

The Pennant indicates:

1. A stock's value will start to grow or fall sharply. The change could be for the stock to gain or lose a few percentage points of its value. The change should be noticeable, however valuable it may be.

2. The value then should start going in the opposite direction. After a sizeable increase, it will slowly decrease, or it could go the other way around.

3. The values of the stock rises or drops will shrink in size after a time. With each candlestick, a stock could change by just a few pennies in value. Sometimes the total volume or range within which the value of the stock changes in a period of time may be minimal.

4. The stock will have little to no variation in its value after a while.

5. When the stock suddenly breaks out, the pennant will end and experience an increase or decrease in its value. This should be a complete continuation of what the stock had been experiencing before the pennant began.

The pennant's layout will let you know that the value of stock either stabilizes or is about to erupt. When the volume of trading and the value change shrinks to next to nothing, this is a sign that something is about to happen. Sometimes, depending on how the pennant started, you might find that the value could go up or down after a while.

Enter a pennant when you notice changes coming down to very low totals in each wave. Watch how the pennant is formed, and see how it breaks out of stock. On the opposite end of the trend, you can place a stop-loss order to protect you against the stock's potential, not continuing in the same path or if the pennant lasts a bit longer than expected.

Bullish or Bearish?

A pennant can either be bullish or its value bearish. A bullish pennant is one that begins on a slight rally. In the beginning, the stock price will go up and then stabilize. The stock will probably shift back up in value once the pennant is formed.

A bearish pennant features a price that falls substantially before the pennant forms. The price may start to go up a bit, but after the pennant ends, the value will go down. You could probably say the same about any other pattern that you find. The pattern changes are all worth checking to anticipate that certain changes might grow and evolve.

The Flag – a Related Pattern

A pennant may occasionally occur in a more rectangular shape. That is, the value doesn't necessarily increase or decrease by much, but remains within a steady range. This establishes a flag pattern, which is in a flag-shaped pattern with the candlesticks on a chart moving. Whether the flag is bullish or bearish, you can still identify by looking at how it started. The first few price changes in the flag should give you an idea of how the flag moves in value up or down.

Think of the flag as if it were a series of oscillating waves throughout, with the same amplitude. The only difference is that the time periods on that wave will vary between the highs and lows. Ultimately, when you notice a sizable breakout from the flag, you would have to enter your trade.

Can the Pennant Go in the Other Direction?

Most pennants are made to go right to the left. That is, the biggest change in price will appear on the left while the smallest will go to the right. There are times when you can form an inverse pennant. This is where the volume of trading and changes in stock begin to gradually increase, eventually transforming into one big trade at the end of the pennant.

Not as easy to find reverse pennants as traditional ones. You will find a reverse pennant more likely after it's finished. Sometimes these reverse pennants might let you know how the price moves and how the stock is about bullish or bearish people. Just look at the ends of the reverse pennants, you'll get an idea of how a stock is developing.

Strategies for Using Pennants

You should use some strategies on the market to trad pennants:

Watch how the changes in the candlesticks vary as the pennant advances. Sometimes a majority of sticks move up in the pennant. They may, in other cases, go downwards. Either way, after the pennant is fully formed, it might be better for you to get into commerce. You might try to make small micro-transactions that last for a few minutes depending on where the pennant flows, but even then, it may be hard to determine how long the waves will move along and how many up or down candlesticks will form at a time. Seek out as many pennants as possible in stock. Reviewing multiple pennants gives you an insight into what a stock sentiment might be. You could see bullish pennants growing bigger. This suggests investors are more appreciative of stock and willing to make investments in it.

Trade, where possible, during stock upside parts. Trading at this point helps as you identify points where a stock's value will likely rise in a shorter period of time. This would work only for a brief moment before something begins to shrink in value.

See if a pennant contains any significant outliers. These include cases in which one stick is larger in the middle than the other. An outlier is suggestive of stock uncertainty. It shows when the outliner moves downwards that a possible increase may not be as strong as it might be. Look at how long a pennant may be on the move. The pennant may sometimes last for a couple of days or even some weeks at a time. A pennant could last for a few hours, in most cases. This is because people will respond swiftly to stock changes. They might notice that a stock that trends upward and is stable in value might be worthwhile acquiring before the value might burst up again.

Wedge

The following pattern is a wedge. This is akin to the pennant, but it uses a different form. A wedge is a pattern where the wave of price reverses. After a while, the range in a stock's price will begin to narrow. The stock will break out after the wedge ends and move up or down.

What distinguishes the coin from a pennant? A wedge is organized within a certain range based on the differences between stock prices. An example of how a wedge can be formed here is:

1. You may notice a trend where a stock's price moves up and down and then down again. A stock could start at $100, for example, and then move up to $120 after a few days. After a few more days, the stock would then fall to $105.

2. The extremes are beginning the wedge between the first values. Just like with a pennant, the wedge will feature two lines. The first line begins at the $120 part, and the other begins at the $100 mark.

3. The wedge lines will move inward, based on stock range changes. You might notice the stock will go from $105 to $115 and then to $112 in a couple of days. As the gap between price extremes begins to shrink, the lines will become narrow.

4. The wedge will shrink to where the price may appear to break out after some time. By looking at how the wedge began, you can identify whether the wedge is bullish or bearish. If the wedge

started with the price moving up, then there's a chance the price will break out after the wedge ends.

The Three Types of Wedges

The main strategy to use when trading wedges is to look at how the wedges are organized. There are three shapes of wedges that you might notice, with each being different based on how a stock's value is going to change over time:

1. Rising wedge-This is where the highs and lows of the wedge keep moving up. You can tell when the wedge is rising that the stock is about to trend downward. You will have to sell your stock when the low on a rising wedge breaks beyond the lower bar. This is a sign that the stock is about to take a dramatic decline in value and possibly move further downward. This could occasionally lead to a falling wedge. This is the next wedge.

2. Wedge falling-The wedge falling is the opposite of the wedge rising. The ups and downs continue to decline. You

should buy the stock from the top part of the wedge when it breaks out.

3. Symmetrical wedge-A symmetrical wedge has a relatively similar design to a pennant. But the gap's narrowing won't be as close as it would be to a pennant. You can see if the wedge will move up or down when you notice how the wedge started. This is just like a pennant as a wedge, which begins to increase in value and will surely continue to rise.

These three wedges are designed with different arrangements, but they are all vital to help you see where a stock could be going. Reviewing the wedge layout is vital to trying to get a trade option ready, which is the next item to look into here.

Take Profits on Options

The take profit should be analyzed if you have a wedge-based trade option. The profit from taking refers to the starting point of a wedge. When the rising wedge begins, it is high at the start of the falling wedge or the low. You can order an option that lasts for a certain period of time and is geared towards making a profit. At this point, the best strategy is to decide how long a wedge will develop. This might give you an idea of how long the option that you wish to place might be. You should keep the option long enough to give the stock the chance to return to the point of profit-taking.

This is irrespective of how long it might take to move the wedge.

Cup and Handle

The cup and handle have an intriguing shape, which you will notice quickly. This can indicate not only a continuation of a stock's value but also a reversal. More relevantly, this shows a stock's value will rise after a brief dip. In the end, as the pattern ends, the value of the stock will move up in value. The cup and handle are arranged in three parts. They are focusing heavily on dramatic market changes:

1. The Cup-This is where stock value begins to bend in value. At the start, it will dip below a certain value and then

move back to around the value it was when the cup began.

2. The Handle-The handle is a line that shows up around the cup end. This is a line that shows a slight downtrend. This is comparable to what you might see from a downward-moving pennant or wedge.

3. A breakout-After the handle is finished, the breakout appears. The breakout happens when the stock value begins to rise beyond what the handle is showing.

This is an intriguing organization, showing how the value of a stock could change. What is very interesting is that the pattern of the cup and handle might repeat itself several times over.

How Deep Can the Decline Be?

The cup and handle decline should not exceed 50 percent. Be aware of this may be a sign that a stock is in real danger when planning and developing as a decline of more than 50 percent. In case it goes too deep, it would be harder for a stock to recover. More importantly, it is an indication of general instability or insecurity among investors regarding how that stock could perform and evolve.

Reversal Pattern

In a reversal or continuation layout, you can find a cup and handle the trend in one stock. Let's look at those points first:

1. The stock price must be falling. -- The stock should have fallen in the last few weeks or months.

2. A sizeable decline is beginning to develop. The decline that begins the cup should be bigger and more consistent than the preceding declines.

3. In the middle of the cup should be a couple of small candlesticks that don't change much in value. That should be a sign that the stock is moving upward.

4. The stock then starts recovering and reaches the other end of the cup. The cup's two ends should be equal in value.

The cup shape will vary, but the ends will have to be the same.

5. A handle will be formed for a short time with the stock going down in value.

The handlebars are subjective. The bars can be positioned in any way you think fit.

6. As with a pennant or wedge, the stock finally breaks out of the handle and moves upward in value. The stock should continue to an upward trend. Your method at this moment is to look at how well they handle formed to make a purchase while waiting for the stock to break out.

Continuation Pattern

The pattern of continuation is similar in a way to a reversal, in that the stock is going to go down, up and down, and up again. The variation here is that while a reversal involves the stock going down before the cup and handle start, the continuation pattern occurs when the stock rises in value before the formation.

By looking at any significant decreases in the uptrend, you can identify when the cup starts. You might notice some small-sized candlesticks followed by a large red one that goes down. Here the cup should start.

An Option Target Point

You can use the cup and handle trade options to give you an idea of what the target should be. With a few steps, you can calculate the target for a trade of options:

1. Revise the cup's height. The height is the difference between the cup's start and endpoint and the lowest total value. Let's say the cup started and ended at $6, and the stock dropped to midway through $4.50. At this point, the cup should be at $1.50 in height.

2. Add the height of the cup on the handle to the breakout point. The stock may have a handle that falls down to $5.50 before the stock breaks out, after reaching $6 as the cup ends. Add the $1.50 to the $5.50 to get to $7.

3. At this point, the price target should be shaped. The price target of $7 can be used as a goal for options trades to reach your option. At some point in the future, you could contract to buy a stock at $7 and then sell it with a sizeable profit if the stock is valuable much more than $7. You'd need to look at how long it can take to reach the target.

Of course, at this juncture, you have the option of just engaging in traditional trade. If you feel it will take a while for the trade to move on, you could do this.

Added Cup and Handle Trading Strategies

For your investment plans, there are a few extra strategies to use when getting a cup and handling trade:

Review how well-shaped the handle is. A shorter handle is a positive sign. The stock is moving up very soon. A handle could possess a minimum number of sticks. There's a better overall sentiment among traders about a stock when the handle is shorter. This suggests the stock is fast moving up. This could be perfect if you want to engage in a short-term trade. When you look at how the rally moves, you'd have to be cautious and if it could stop fast.

Use a target price that is up to at most two cup heights over the long term. For long-term trading, the best idea is to use two cup heights for how the stock will move up in value. The cup and handle should suggest the stock is moving up in value and becoming interesting to investors. Staying at just two cup heights is best as it reduces your risk and keeps your expectations under control. This also prevents you from losing too much in case the stock doesn't continue to move up in value.

Place a stop-loss command at the bottom of your handle. Although the risk of the stock going below the bottom of the handle is minimal, in the event that the stock continues to decline, you should still add a stop-loss order around that point.

When the handle starts, a short sale can work, but you'd have to watch out for its length. When the handle is formed, you can sell short of taking advantage of the drop in stock value. Note that a handle will last only for a few candlesticks at a time. Keep in your short sale about three to five sticks, so you can take advantage of the decline before any dramatic shifts occur.

Is This a Guarantee a Stock Will Actually Go Up?

Although the pattern of cup and handle shows a stock's value will go up, there is still a chance that stock will experience a significant decline. The best way to tell when the stock risks decreasing afterward is to notice how deep the cup is. This is a signal of how strong the movement could be and whether any gains on this investment could be difficult to maintain or support.

A cup with a very small dip has a greater chance of falling in value than a stock with a deeper dip. A handle that is also very narrow in size may also later decrease or at least take some time for it to recover and move up in value.

Can the Handle Move Upward?

There are times when the handle will actually move up in value on a cup and handle. This is a sign that a stock is favored by people, but you still have to be careful. A handle upward is only going to have very small increases. Some declines may appear after the handle, but at this point, the stock should still be moving upward. It may not move as fast and require you to stay with a longer trade, but it might be worth looking into.

An upward handle also may suggest that after the pattern is finished, a stock will not increase its value by as much as one might expect it. A lot of the trade will have already taken place during the formation of the cup and handle. At this juncture, the public may not be as bullish on the stock as they notice that its growth rate has stalled.

Head and Shoulders

One of the most common features you'll see in a stock is the pattern of the head and shoulders. It consists of six trends in a stock that goes in opposite directions of one another. The value of the stock may change, but it always returns to a pivot point. At the beginning of the head and shoulders trend, that point is formed and, at the very end, will be the same. It's around the point your strategy should come into play as you make a trade based on where the stock is about to move and how far it is going to go in that direction. The stock will break out when the head and shoulder pattern ends. It'll continue to move in a particular direction. There are two viewable positions in the pattern of the head and shoulders:

Top Position

The first position is the head and the top of the shoulders. This is a bearish pattern showing the stock is going to fall in value giving traders the belief that the stock is going to continue declining.

In the head and top of the shoulders, there are six points to see with each part of the definite pattern a distinct segment of the human body:

1. The left shoulder occurs when a rising stock's value is about to fall in value or is stuck at the same total.

2. The first pullback happens when the value of the stock drops and is ready to go up.

3. When the stock moves up, the head is formed and is then about to decline. The head-on position should always be the highest point.

4. The stock will revert to the first pullback value. The second pullback forms this.

5. After the stock price moves up again, the right shoulder is formed and stays put for a little before falling. The right shoulder may be higher than the left shoulder or lower.

6. The breakout occurs when the stock price goes under the pullback mark and continues to decline.

Trading the Top

A useful strategy for this top position layout of the head and shoulders is to put a short-trade around the breakout level. At the breakout level, you can sell shares and then repurchase them shortly after when the stock starts to decay. Before the downward trend becomes more pronounced, the value will keep going back to or over the breakout point. You can also see how quickly the stock's value could begin to decline. You might see cases where the value of the stock is steady, but every once in a while it will experience slight declines. This can be used when planning trade-in options, so you know when to place a put order.

Using the Price Target

A good strategy for a place option on top of the head and shoulders is to place an order regarding the price target you set in this case. Here is what you can do to help you get this to work:

1. Take the right shoulder and extract it from the point of breakout.

2. At this point, you should have the head and shoulders high.

3. From breakout, subtract the height.

4. The result is the target that you have for the stock value decrease.

A stock with a $35 right shoulder and a $30 breakout, for instance, will have a $5 high. To get to the $25 price target for a put option, this should be subtracted from $30. This should be the mark you would like to get the stock down to when you invest in this option.

Also, you have the option to play percentages when you set a price target:

1. Review the right shoulder decline to the breakout point.

2. Calculate the decline-percentage. In the above example, as it goes from $35 to $30, the stock will have declined by about 15 percent.

3. Set a target under the breakout point based on the percentage total. The target would be 15 percent below $30 at this

point. The target is set to be around $25.50.

You can use either of those options to set the price point. The total will be near the same, whatever you choose.

Bottom Position

The bottom position is the next thing for measurement calculation. The setup of the bottom head and shoulders is, in essence, the reverse of the top position:

1. At the start, the stock will go down in value.

2. The left shoulder is formed around the end of a pattern in which the value descends.

3. When the stock moves back up in value, the pullback positions occur.

4. The head is still to be lower than anything else in value.

5. The stock should move into the breakout point after moving back to the pullback position for the second time and

then forming the right shoulder. The breakout point should be fully surpassed at this juncture, as the stock is starting to rise in value.

For the head and shoulders bottom, you can use the same target price measurement as what you use for the top. When calculating that price point, you can use either this same difference between the right shoulder and the breakout or the percentage difference between the two.

The setup at the bottom is perfect for a call option. See how the stock responds when it decides on the correct target price.

Trading Ideas For Head and Shoulders

Waiting for the pattern to complete itself before you enter a position is the most effective technique to use when trading the head and shoulders pattern. You should never assume the pattern continues all the way through. The earliest you might consider trading this pattern is to trade or launch the option around the top right shoulder part. This is around the time when the stock trend should go in the direction that you expect it to.

After the breakout point is reached, you can also wait for a few spots to see where the stock moves. Look at how fast it may take the stock to move to a certain point and that it does not struggle in any way. When you get the head and shoulders pattern to work for you, you have to be cautious.

Triangles

The next pattern to look at is the pattern with the triangle. It is a pattern of continuation, although it can sometimes be a pattern of reversal. When the price changes in stock start to narrow, a triangle develops. Here is a basic idea of how a triangle might be formed:

1. A triangle starts right as the stock heads down or up in worth over a few periods of trading.

2. Eventually, the stock returns in the opposite direction. This forms the line, which constitutes the other part of the triangle.

3. The stock is continuing to move back and forth. As the stock moves, the differences between the back and out points will be smaller.

4. The triangle is finally formed to perfection. There should be a breakout at this point where the stock is moving in the direction it was going at the triangle starts.

As the highs and lows of the stocks form, the triangle continues to alternate and become smaller in value. A triangle could show stock with $35, $30, and $25 highs with multiple points of $15, $20, and $22. That means the triangle shows a spread overtime of $20, $10, and $3. Such shrinking spreads will form the triangle and reveal the stock's potential to break out of the pattern. The breakout point is vital as it indicates when the earlier trend continues. It is here where it is possible to order an options trade or a straightforward stock purchase.

Triangles are popular among investors because the potential for reward and risk is about the same. People may use stop-loss commands near a triangle's opposite end to keep their losses from being too intense. In the meantime, examining how well the form of the triangle gives the investor an idea of how a stock could potentially increase its value.

The triangle shows no matter what happens, a trend is very resistant. That trend will continue to move in the same direction it had initially moved in. This shows a sense of consistency regarding how the stock is moving.

How the Triangle is Different from a Pennant

The triangle shape is clearly similar to what you'd see on a pennant. A pennant indicates the value of a stock moving briefly in the opposite direction of a continuing pattern. A triangle shows the stock moving inside the same value without much change of value experienced by the stock. It is essentially a pattern delay, except that there are no significant changes in the value of the triangle.

Can a Reversal Happen?

A triangle has the potential of showing a reversal in a stock's trend and appearing not as likely as a continuing trend. See how the triangle closes and how the stock continues to change in value. Sometimes a stock with multiple candlesticks in the triangle going the other way of the original trend could cause a reversal because the momentum is beginning to pick up where the stock is going in a different direction over time.

Three Kinds of Triangles

There are three specific kinds of triangles that you will see forming in a stock. These are separated according to how the stock's value may change at one or both ends. These show similar changes to what you'd find in other patterns.

1. Symmetric Triangle-The symmetric triangle is one in which the lines move toward one another. This forms the pennant-like shape that shows that inside the stock you hold, there might be some sort of even movement.

2. Ascending Triangle-When the lower line is rising, an ascending triangle occurs, but the upper line is at a consistent value. For example, the highs could be $30, $31, and $29.50, while the lows would be $22, $26, and $28. The stock's swings are getting smaller in value, but the stock doesn't necessarily move up. This type of triangle is a sign that the stock will probably decrease in value. You can set the breakthrough point a little earlier than if you prefer the triangle should end. You may notice when stock will peak.

3. Descending Triangle-The downward triangle is the opposite of the upward triangle. It shows the stock will more than likely continue to move in value.

The lows are all at the same peaks, while the highs keep shrinking before the stock finally breaks out.

Determining the Target Price

When placing a trade from a triangle, the target price for an options call or a put should be carefully measured. There are a few steps to be employed:

1. First, set a stop-loss at the triangle's bottom or top part. The positioning should be determined on the basis of trends in the stock. If the stock is moving up in value, place the stop-loss at the bottom. Do the opposite of ever weaker stock.

2. Measure the height from the bottom of the triangle end to the top of the start. For example, the top part could be at $40, while the bottom might be at $30; at this point, the total is $10.

3. Subtract or add that total from or to your breakout point.

In the example, the target price should be $50 for a call option. A put option should have a 20 dollar target. The overall goal is to look at how the bars move within the triangle and how the stock will change. This gives you a better chance of investing in quality whilst understanding how strong a stock could develop over time.

Double Top or Bottom

The top and bottom doubles are a popular pattern of reversal. This shows a stock will head high or low but will not go too far beyond the listed peaks. The stock will go in the opposite direction after reaching those peaks from where it had been moving.

How the Double Top Is Formed

The double top features a stock that at first trends upward:

1. It will eventually reach the first stop as the stock moves up in value. That's the highest value the stock will attain.

2. The stock then pulls back in value. There are no standards on how much of

a difference between the pullback value and the first top should be found.

3. Then the stock rallies back up to reach the second top, which should be about as high as the first.

4. The stock then moves down to its original low pullback.

5. There may be a chance that the stock will begin to move up in value or stay the same, but the stock will eventually break below that total pull back, thus completing the double top.

The double top can give an idea of when a stock might be traded, as it is within the pattern. This pattern works particularly well if you want to put an option onto the stock. Look at how this is where the second top is formed. This is the point where a short sale or a put option can be entered.

How the Double Bottom is Formed

The double bottom is formed in the very same fashion as the double top but the other way round:

- The double bottom starts when there's a downward trend in the stock.
- Twice, the stock will appear to be reaching its lowest total.
- The stock will move far beyond pullback value after a while and begin to go up in value.
- The double bottom is perfect for calling options. When you review the trend, you will notice how the stock is about to rise in value.

Selecting a Price Target

Regardless of whether you buy and sell the double bottom or top, you can set a price target for anything that you want to invest in. Here's how to set a target price:

1. See where the top and bottom doubles are formed. You could see, for example,

that the double tops on a stock are at $45 and $44.

2. Use the point between the two peaks at midway. You'll be using $44.50 as one border for this.

3. Consider where the trend's opposite ends are located. Get the point at midway between those two. The bottom parts that appear after the double tops, in the example, are around $35 and $33. So the midway would be $34.

4. Find the difference between the two totals which you've collected. Subtract $34 off $44.50 to reach a $10.50 difference.

5. Add or subtract the total to or from the point of breakout. Since the double tops show the stock is going to go down in value, you have to take $10.50 off the breakout. The second bottom part was $33, so let's use that as the mark for a breakout. The target price you should use then would be $22.50.

In short, you'd put an option on the price that goes under $22.50. You could also use this as a means of seeing if the stock is going to rally at the $22.50 mark if they get there. Either way, you have to work with a benchmark to identify how the value of the stock will change.

Where to Create a Stop-Loss

When you get a stop-loss planned on your double bottom or a top stock trade, you have two options to work with:

1. Creates a stop-loss between the breakout point and tops or bottoms at the midway point. You would use a stop-loss total of roughly $38.50 for the double top example listed above. This is in between the top $44 and the breakout label of $33.

2. You can also opt for a stop-loss around the top or bottom double spot. A $44 stop-loss could be used to stop you from losing anything in case the stock exceeds that original peak.

You have the option to store the stop-loss at other stock values if you wish. These two options are recommended because they are less risky.

Space Between Each Top or Bottom

To see how it is developing, look at the number of candlesticks in a double top or bottom pattern. A good trading pattern in between the bottom or top and the opposite end should have about four to seven sticks. This indicates how the stock tries to pass a certain total but struggles to do so. This also shows that traders have some sense of control due to consistent top and bottom swings. If you start noticing that the spacing between the top and bottom parts is consistent, you might feel more confident in a trade.

Can a Triple Top or Bottom Occur?

It is possible that a double top or bottom could have three peaks or valleys instead of two. This will not always be the case, but when you consider how the double top or bottom might clearly show a sense of uncertainty among investors, it is a possibility.

The third peak or valley will be slightly off the first two, in a triple top or bottom. The first two tops on a triple top could be $50 and $52, while the third top would be $46. This is a noticeable shift from the others and adds some confirmation that the stock will head in the opposite direction from where it first moved. There'll not always be triple tops or bottoms. If that happens, then the third instance will not be very intense.

Pocket Pivot

The pocket pivot is a distinct feature you might see in a stock. This happens when, after a consistent decrease or rise, the stock experiences a slight change in its value. You might notice, for example, five or more candlesticks where the stock either continues to go down or has an extremely minimal increase. Anyway, the stock would fall. You'll see a significant rise in the stock's value on the sixth candlestick. That rise may be small, but still noteworthy. In a pocket pivot pattern, there are three things that need to be noticed:

1. The inventory needs to go in the opposite direction.

2. At this juncture, the change in stock value should be significant. It should be higher in value than the changes that had come before it on the candlesticks. For example, on one stick, a stock might have declined by 40 cents, and then on the next by 50. The pocket point shows the stock is 60 cents up.

3. The volume of trade on the stock should be higher than in the last few trading periods. The best pocket pivots occur when the volume is nearly twice what it was before the pivot happened.

Compared to other investments, this is a rather small pattern and one that can repeat itself on a chart many times over. You may see a pocket pivot occurring every few days or even every few hours. This is because a cycle is set up in which people are willing to buy the stock and then quickly sell it off. A pocket pivot shows the stock in question is well-controlled, and the investors get an idea of what they want to do with it. Use this part of a trade to see how a stock moves, and you get an idea of where it is going to be heading.

A stop-loss order may be applied where necessary to the opposite end of the pivot point. This is enough to maintain control whilst attaining a decent value.

Each of these patterns shows that a stock can move in many directions on a stock market chart. Be aware of how these patterns establish so you can have an idea of not only where a stock will head but also how the prices might change within a pattern.

Chapter 7: Buying Stocks on Margin

You might want to make a trade, but maybe you don't have the money to do it. This is fine, as many brokers will enable you to buy stocks marginally. Margin-buying is a simple concept. To pay for a trade you wish to complete, you borrow money from a broker. You're going to be using that money to buy more stock shares. You could also use the money to access a very expensive stock you couldn't normally afford. Margin trading is a risky strategy, and it's so risky that you might not be able to make a margin account with some investment brokers unless you have a history with that broker. To properly know how margin trading works, you must follow a couple of specific rules.

1. You will need to apply for a margin account to get started. A margin account differs from that of a cash account.

2. You must also sign a margin agreement and agree to the terms for margin trading, which a broker set. This should include information about how large a trade margin can be and what the trade rate is.

3. You can do a deal. You could have $20,000 in a margin account, for example. You might see a stock valued at $400 per share. You might ask to buy that stock from 100 shares. That would need $40,000, though.

4. The amount of money in your account will go toward the part of the cost after you make the trade, while the rest is a broker's loan.

5. At some point, you'll need to pay back the total value of that loan. That will include margin-rate interest. That makes it all the more important to look at that stock's performance. You can always sell the stock at the right time and cover the loan and interest costs. This only works when you step into a successful position.

6. You'll also need totals to your margin. Your margin account may have certain limits on what you are able to borrow at a time.

Margin Rates

The margin rate is the interest charged on a loan from a broker. Going back to the previous example, you might have been given a 7 percent rate on a margin of $20,000. That means you'll have to pay an interest of $1,400 on the margin trade. The rate is determined by the broker which you are using. For example, for people who deposit less than $25,000 into their margin accounts, Charles Schwab has a margin rate of 8.575 percent. That number is reduced to 7.075 percent for $100,000 accounts and then to 6.825 percent for $250,000 or more accounts. Merrill Edge charges 9,625 percent for $25,000 or less accounts and $100,000 for 7,125 per cent.

The good news about margin trading is that usually, you can borrow up to 50 percent of the total value of the position you want to enter. This is the maximum, which is typical. New margin traders should be able to borrow about 25 percent of their portfolio total. A new trader with a budget of $20,000 could buy about $5,000 in margin-processed trades. Often this limit is used because a person may not have enough margin trading experience. The broker who offers this deal just keeps the risk under control. It's becoming easier to do more with more buying power. You may be given a higher total margin to work with as you have more money in your account, and you continue to be profitable with margin trades. That can get you to the 50 percent value you're aiming for. You might try to buy $10,000 in stock, for example. You may have $5,000 you want to use in cash to pay for the investment. The other amount could be an offer on the margins.

A margin trading company could have limits on how much money you can spend on the trade. For example, you might need to have $15,000 or more in an account to trade in $10,000 on a margin trade. Such rules are applied by trading firms to ensure that people have the necessary funds to carry out trades and repay the loan and any margin-related charges if the trade goes south.

Examples

The following are examples for both again on a margin trade and a loss.

When a Gain Occurs

1. You have a $30,000 Margin Account.

2. You see a stock you would like to buy, but you need to use a margin. In particular, you want to get $150 worth of 100 shares of stock trading. You'd have to spend 15,000 dollars on commerce. For a margin trade, you can always use a part of your $30,000.

3. You are going to have to spend $7,500 on initial trade, and the other $7,500 is going to be on the margin. The margin would have a 7.5 percent interest rate. The interest rate again varies depending on the broker and how much you have put into your margin requirement.

4. When you decide to sell the trade, the stock increases to $190 in value. That $15,000 investment now has a value of $19,000.

5. Along with interest on the loan, you must repay the $7,500 margin. In this example, the interest would be $562.50.

6. From this trade, you'll have made a profit of $3,437.50. The profit is based on how the value of your original $7,500 grew to $9,500. The interest would be withdrawn from commerce. You'll have realized a substantial profit in the end.

This particularly illustrates how, when you work with a margin, you could get a greater profit from a successful trade. Just 50 shares of stock would have been a trade like this without margin. The $7,500 you are investing would turn into $9,500. You would have earned $2,000 from this trade, but that's far less than you'd realized if you'd used a margin trade involving more shares. This is why so many people love to trade margins. They love it is a practice that gives them a greater chance of making a bigger profit than using their own money.

When a Loss Occurs

Obviously, you need a margin trade to be successful in making a profit. The losses that could result from trade-in margins if the stock does not increase in value.

1. You paid $200 for 100 shares of a stock with $10,000 coming from your own account and $10,000 coming from a margin loan. This would also include an interest rate of 7.5 percent.

2. Before you sell the shares, the stock goes down to $150

3. You'll only realize $15,000 if you sell the shares.

4. You must pay back the margin loan of $10,000 plus the interest charge of $750.

5. That results in a $4.250 loss.

Now let's say you went with a straight cash transaction in which you got 50 shares without using a margin for purchasing 100 shares. You'll invest $10,000 in the stock and then sell it to $7,500 for a $2,500 loss. If you spent more money on your margin trade, the potential for you to lose money could be even worse. What is more, if the stock falls further, the damage would be even worse.

For Which Stocks Can You Use Margins?

Please be advised that with each stock, you cannot use margin trades. You can't use margin trades on initial public offerings, penny stocks, or other stocks that could be considered highly risky.

The Board of the Federal Reserve determines which stocks may be marginally tradable. The Board will decide how those stocks are to be used based on various factors, such as how much money is involved, among other factors. The Board's aim is to prevent investors from spending too much money on risky inventories.

Margin Calls

Margin calls are used when the value of stock spikes when you want more cash available. If a stock is making a dramatic decrease, you may need to pay more cash or stock to cover the losses involved. In the meantime, if the price has a huge positive spike, you might be asked to pay the broker back. This is to allow the broker to have the funds available on short notice for managing the trade.

A margin call's total value should be about 10-20 percent of the total investment. That does not mean that there is absolutely going to be a margin call. The best strategy to use here is to look at how the stock has moved and looked at any case where the stock has experienced a dramatic fall in value.

Strategies for Margin Trading

Margin trading is a great way to make more money, but it is only experienced traders who should make margin trades. The potential for a profit could be enormous, but the margin involved can also aggravate any loss you encounter. You can use a few margin trading strategies to keep potential losses from becoming a burden. These focus more on keeping a sense of control.

Keep Your Margins Small at the Start

Just because you could at the beginning get twice the size of an investment when using a large margin trade doesn't mean that's the best idea. You must keep your margins in check whilst at the start using your own money. For example, in the beginning, you can stay with a 10 percent margin. This keeps the danger of a margin trade lower while providing you with a sensible introduction to how those trades work. A smaller trade margin is best when the stock that you want to trade is slightly more unstable. A stock that can change in value in less than a week by 10 percent or more should only be purchased with smaller margins.

Look for Stop Orders

For margin trades, stoppage orders are even more important. You can use a stop order to keep the failures down, but looking at how such orders work for-profits might be even more important. It is best to add a stop order a little over your stock's original value, as this ensures that any margin calls that might occur are minimized.

Avoid Speculation

It's also critical that when looking at what might actually occur with a stock, you avoid any kind of speculation. Speculation is problematic in that it makes an emotional decision easier for a person. This expects a stock to possibly move up in value without actually looking at various factors linked to the stock history.

High Rewards Mean Higher Risks

Although you can understand a profit from your marginal trades, as you would have been able to buy more stocks, this is still a very risky endeavor. As with any type of investment, when the reward is also great, the risk is greater. Because you trade on the margin, you work with more shares than you might otherwise have been able to buy. You are expanding your buying ability, but you also risk losing money.

In short, margin trades are exciting because they can give you a better chance of making a big profit. You also need to watch the value of a stock carefully and how it could change as the losses could be even worse.

Review with the broker you wish to use the terms of the margin trades.

Chapter 8: How to Identify Bad Stock News

We are living in a time when it's very easy to mislead people. We look at social media stories that claim to be real, and we assume they are accurate, but in reality, those stories are just rumors or falsehoods that random people spread about. Perhaps the worst false stories relate to certain stock investments. You may hear stuff about stocks worth investing in, but that information may not be correct. Those news stories may sometimes suggest that something could happen that will cause a stock to drop in value. Sometimes those who want to manipulate stocks are planted by the reports. Often many traders make deals based on a fake news story. Be careful to read any news story. There are several tips you can use to identify bad news stories so that it doesn't mislead your investment strategies.

Social Media Is Risky

The first sign that the news story stocks is when it is published on a social media website. The problem with finding these tips on social media sites is that those sites are often filled with fake accounts that people like running. Some people like to spread rumors. You can tell that a stock tip on social media that you find is bad if:

The person posting that message is anonymous.

You are also unknown about the organization, which claims this tip is useful. I could not verify the group responsible for posting this on a social media site. An unverified account is one that nobody, in particular, can confirm to hold.

The tip listed could include misrepresentations, inaccuracies, or other errors. These fundamental errors, such as referring to Cedar Fair stock as having the symbol CF instead of its actual symbol FUN, suggest somebody is rushing to post something online and has no accurate information.

Do your own due diligence to see if there's a stock worth it. Look online to see if the stock in question is legitimate and if the tip information can be confirmed through stock review.

Avoid Anonymous Sources

When reading stock tips, one thing you might hear involves anonymous sources stating certain items about a stock. You might hear stuff about a stock being a good deal, or perhaps something about a company that might impact a stock's value. Do not believe anything from sources that are anonymous. May not be legitimate, many sources claiming anonymity. These include sources that may not have a direct understanding of the stock over which they are posting rumors. Sometimes a news source may take an anonymous tip without considering the impacts, or maybe they have further motives to post the rumor

Who Else Is Reporting?

You might find at times that nobody else reports on a specific stock. You might see that no one wants to discuss stock-related things based on value changes, acquisitions with which a company could be working, and so on.

You may come across a stock tip listed on some site as an "exclusive" tip. That place could be claiming it's the only place you'll get that information. Did that entity has claimed other exclusives in the past? Have great stock-investment stories been released before? Be aware of any person reporting stories that nobody else is discussing and is certainly not a story you would like to trust. You never know where the story might have originated. After all, that "exclusive" label could be just a case of somebody trying to say something interesting and having no basis in truth.

Review the Fine Print

In any news story you read, you have to look at the fine print no matter in which stock you want to invest. A news story will sometimes say the stock tips come from a person who was paid to disseminate that information. A case where compensation is given to someone for offering tips needs to be disclosed in a report. It's often a sign of concern, as the news report could just be a promotional advertisement for a stock.

Additionally, there are times when a person who writes a story says he or she has some position to discuss with the stock. One person who holds that stock could write a story about Boeing stock. At the bottom of the story, that writer must state that he or she holds some stock in Boeing. This suggests the writer may be biased and maybe trying to hide information that could hurt the stock's value. They need to take storylines like this with a grain of salt. The writer might, after all, just write a positive-sounding series of stories because that person wants to push the stock to a more advantageous position for him.

Where to Find News

Although it's easy to fall for fake stock-related news stories, you don't have to constantly struggle with those issues. For stock news, you can go to various useful places. Here are some of the best places to consider when retrieving stock news:

Investopedia regularly offers information about various trading events and service providers. Simulators are also available to assist you in reviewing how stocks trade. The site does well to report margin trading, options trading, and many other investment firms.

Yahoo Finance focuses on specifics when reporting on inventories. It includes information on how stocks are traded on the basis of volume, P / E ratio, and many other technical considerations.

For a long time, the Wall Street Journal has been a reliable option for financial information. The Journal can be found throughout the country on newsstands and can be shipped to your home, but that does cost money to get regular access to what the WSJ offers.

Thanks to its solid platform, Bloomberg is a popular name for business news. It also offers various reports which are based on certain markets. Bloomberg's information is detailed and gives you all you need to know about a stock.

Do not forget to check what your stock screener or trading broker could offer. They must include detailed and regularly updated information from the sources noted above and from others. Look for your own additional information too.

There are plenty of legitimate sources that offer details of quality from which you can profit. False information is plentiful, but if you simply know where to go to find legitimate information, you do not have to struggle with it.

Chapter 9: Penny Stocks

The stocks you read about here are the ones that are expensive to invest in. You don't need to stay with those expensive inventories. You are given the option to select penny stocks. Penny stocks are stocks of firms trading at very low values. The SEC says a penny stock is worth less than $5 per share and will not be listed on one of the major exchanges. Penny stocks sound interesting on the surface because they are so cheap. At the same time, these investments are risky and difficult to work with, because when you trade them, it's impossible to figure out where they might go. There are some things that you can do to successfully trade them out.

What Is a Penny Stock?

A penny stock is a stock with a very tiny market cap. Besides having shares of less than $5 each, the company's market cap is worth about $50 million to $300 million and is not necessarily a globally recognized group. There are also some smaller markets where the stock trades. Penny stocks are traded over the counter in the US. That is, the trades are managed without exchange between the parties. Both the OTC Bulletin Board and Pink Sheets list information on how to organize these penny stocks. The most notable feature of penny stocks is that their values are very small. Some of those stocks may not even be worth one centime per stock.

The small real estate company Metro spaces, for example, trades as an OTC stock under the symbol MSPC. Metro spaces had been trading at $0,0001 per share at the beginning of 2018. Not all penny inventories are so cheap. Another OTC stock with the POTN symbol, Pot network Holdings, is a stock of a company dedicated to hemp products. The business has a stock that traded at around 50 cents per share for much of 2018.

The general thing about penny stocks is they're very inexpensive. As you will read next, however, these inventories are extremely risky.

Serious Risks

Hard to Prepare Trades

Many investment brokers aren't going to work with penny stocks, believing they're overly risky and hard to find. They may also be struggling with planning orders because the markets involved are slower than the larger ones. There's also the concern about what happens when a single trade shifts stock value.

No Real Standards

Although many stocks have strong standards of how they are to be traded, in penny stocks, you won't find those. Such a stock doesn't have to meet any significant standards to enter an exchange. An OTC penny stock has no information to file with SEC. The OTCBB does ask that the stocks it lists file with the SEC, but this is not particularly necessary. You can still check the SEC to see if there are proper filings for a stock you want to invest in, but that can be hard to find.

Hard to Find Information

The next issue surrounding OTC penny stocks is that you may not get sufficient details about what's available. You won't find much information about penny stocks, as news agencies won't report about them. These firms are too small to actually take some of these news agencies seriously.

You may want to read information about penny stock tips to check out, including stocks that might fascinate people to invest in. Those reports are often made by people who have positions in those stocks, with heavily biased information. They may also give you symbols and names, but not enough information about what you might expect from those stocks to be realizing. That makes it more difficult for you to actually get the details you need. What is even worse is that it is not easy to access those stocks through a website. If you've tried to type "OTC stock quotes" into a search box, you might just come across a bunch of topics listing details on those quotes. This only helps make penny stocks more unreliable due to the lack of information available in the process.

Do You Know the Businesses Involved?

Check out the Pink Sheets to see some of the currently listed businesses. Recognize any one of these? 've you heard about Nutate Energy Holdings before? What about the holdings of Pazoo or Textmunication? Until now, the odds are you've never even heard of these groups.

Figuring out what makes these businesses tick could be a challenge. When you enter a Pazoo search, you will not see the company's website as the first listing on pazoo.com. Instead, you'll see a bunch of links to sites listing information about how the Pazoo stock works on the market and what trends might be noticed in this penny stock. It would take you a while to figure out that this is a wellness and health group which sells online nutritional products.

This is one of the biggest concerns you need to be aware of regarding investing in penny stocks. While penny stocks may seem intriguing, it's almost impossible to figure out what's popular with the stock or why its value might change.

Easy to Inflate or Adjust

Have you ever noticed cases where a penny stock's value has undergone a dramatic shift within a very short time? For example, Reach Messaging Holdings, an OTC stock underneath the RCMH ticker, experienced a significant, very short-lived bump in its value in February 2018. The value of the stock was $0.0003, but it soon moved to $0.0008. It then went down in just one day to $0.0003, and eventually to $0.0002.

What if, at this point, you had a million shares in RCMH? You might have bought them when the stock was $0.0008 believing the stock would continue to rise. You'd spent $800 on the stock. With that stock falling back to $0.0003, you'd have lost $500 on your capital expenditure. Simply put, you went with the conviction that the stock would continue to rise in value, but that stock actually sagged out.

That RCMH stock could have increased in value because there was a massive trade in that stock by one person. That person may have bought 10 million or more RCMH shares and then sold them off in a couple of hours or days after a sizeable increase in the stock. Even worse, that person could be somebody from within the company. This is a legitimate penny stock problem that many people don't even think about. It just takes one person to inflate or deflate a stock's value. This, in fact, often happens with inventories that are not very liquid. A stock that does not have liquidity will not change much in value unless one individual manages to place a huge order and get a considerable number of shares sold or bought all at once.

Pumping and Dumping

A related issue is the pump and dump strategy with which penny stocks often struggle. Although it isn't illegal, it certainly feels like it should be because it manipulates the value of a penny stock directly and is often done by someone from within the business, such as:

1. A person buys a significant number of shares in a stock. Usually, this is for penny stocks, although theoretically, it could happen with any stock. Many penny stocks lacking volume makes them more likely to be targeted by pump and dump schemes. They manipulate much easier.

2. That person then tries to promote a stock by offering false or potentially misleading statements regarding the ability of the stock to grow. In the past, this was done by phone using cold calling techniques. People can now go to social media or create their own topic writing to promote those stocks.

3. Then people fall for those statements and buy the stock. Usually, the people who choose to buy those stocks are

willing to invest in them without thinking twice. They could be emotionally driven to invest in those stocks and not thoroughly investigate the company.

4. The person who started the scheme will sell off his shares after enough people buy the stocks in question because that person will have made enough money from the people buying the stock.

5. The people who fell from this trick for the pump and dump scheme could lose hundreds or even thousands of dollars. There are very significant problems with the pump and dump scheme.

What if You Do Want to Invest?

You can still invest, if you wish, in penny stocks. The risks of doing so are high, but it doesn't mean they need to be out of bounds. In fact, if you use a few basic strategies, you could earn money from penny stocks or at least reduce the risks involved. Alongside some more in-depth strategies, many of those are common-sense measures.

Do Not Pay Attention to Success Stories

Have you ever come across some site talking about penny stocks and hear someone report he or she has made tens of thousands of dollars in penny stocks trading? This sounds like a great suggestion and encourages you to invest in those stocks. The truth is, success stories like these, as exciting as they are, are often not legitimate. People who claim they made big bucks on penny stock trading are in the absolute minority. These are people who simply went through a few lucky streaks. Knowing what to find in a penny stock is, of course, critical if you are to succeed. There are so many risks and issues on the market, luck is sometimes more important than simply looking up information about what's available on the market. So you should never assume that these success stories will come true for you.

Don't Hold Penny Stocks Too Long

Decide how long your penny stocks will last. You never know when something will change at any given time and can quickly shrink in value.

Look at how stock in Glance Technologies has changed over time. Around the beginning of 2018, GLNNF had a value of $1.40, but in about two months, that stock fell fast to 60 cents.

Many people buy massive quantities of shares in penny stocks, and it's no surprise that people might experience significant losses. After all, many could buy a large number of penny stocks because they're cheap, and more needs to be bought to make a decent profit. If someone holds a stock too long, that person is at risk of having massive drops in the value of the stock.

Buying and selling a penny-stock the same day is perfectly fine. No matter what you do, avoid holding that stock for more than a few days. There's always a chance you'll lose more than you could earn. The lowest stocks should always have a minimum holding time.

When to Sell?

A good strategy for selling penny stocks is to sell them when you have a 20 or 30 percent return. For example, buying 100,000 shares of a stock at $0.01 and then selling them at $0.012 is great, as you go from a total of $1,000 to $1,200. This is an ideal return of 20 percent. Some investors may hold the stocks assuming a stock could really move forward. Someone could assume the same stock will move up to $0.01 at $0.1. Investing in the stock would be extremely difficult to go from $1,000 to $10,000. Even if it did, this would take a very long time to happen. Of course, when they reach a 20 or 30 percent gain threshold, smart investors will have sold their shares anyway, making it nearly impossible for the stock to actually make that huge increase.

On a related note, you should try to add a stop command to your transaction to prevent potential losses from becoming a threat. Then again, some brokerage firms might not actually offer such orders on penny stocks due to the extended risk associated with them. The risk of a pump and dump event might make it so that the actual value goes well beyond what your stop order was for; at that time, you don't want to have a stop order at $0.1 only for the stock to drop to $0.06.

Watch Company Information

Some firms might claim their stocks are growing well. Company management may, however, skew its documents toward the more positive things about a stock. Some of the positive stories might also be inflated to make them sound more interesting and valuable than they really are. Companies are not necessarily required to tell you about their stocks, certain things. They could be working very hard to make their stocks more intriguing for you without revealing any real substance. Always take whatever a company says about its stock and how it changes with a grain of salt, so you don't fall into any investment traps.

Choose Stocks With a High Volume

The next tip is to stay with stocks that have a good volume of trading. These are the inventories people actually buy. These could include stocks traded by a lot of people, thereby reducing the risk of a stock pump and dump scheme. Everything that has at least 100 million trading volumes is always worthwhile. That means that within the last 24 hours of trading, at least 100 million shares were traded.

That tip has one major caveat. You need to look at how the volume changes for a penny stock, based on what is shown in the read-out chart. A chart, for example, could show one or two massive spikes in a stock price. That means one person controlled a great deal of trading. It could, of course, be a sign of a pump and dump attack as well.

It is always easier to trust any stock with a graph or chart that is a little more variable and doesn't have lots of odd shifts in its value.

Avoid Trading More Than Needed

The specific number of penny stock shares that you can purchase could be limitless. While you might be motivated to purchase one million stock shares at a value of $0.0005, that could be a serious risk, in fact. You'd spend $500 on an investment that, if you're not careful, could be going south rather quickly.

On the contrary, try to keep your penny stock holdings from being worth more than a hundred dollars. A better idea is to stay with 100,000 shares at $0.0005. You would only spend $50 on your trade, but at least you won't lose a lot of money if the stock decreases rather than growing as you anticipated.

Never Sell Short

When you think about it, the sale of short sounds like a great idea. You can borrow penny stock shares that appear to have been pumped up, sell them, and then buy back those stocks for a sizeable profit. The truth is that you could lose so much money from the trade than you could afford. For a penny stock, the time period for a short sale could be far too long.

Review Your Position

Consider how your position is organized based on the size of the volume of the stock. Never trade more than 10 percent of the volume of that stock. If you did that, you would end up inflating the stock price. Investing far too much at one time only adds to the overall transaction risk involved. When getting this part of the trade organized, you need to be careful.

When working with penny stocks, remember that you are fully aware of what you're going into in the process. If you are not careful, such stocks could prove to be dangerous and harmful to your investment plans.

Chapter 10: When to Sell a Stock?

Throughout this guide, you have experienced several times when you can reach a stock spot. If it is a strong upward trend or even a tendency indicating a major long-term market shift, the opportunities you have to get into a market are different and worth evaluating just how useful they are. And you'll have to sell your stocks for a bit. Never believe you should hang onto some stock for as much as you want. Instead, when you market something at the right moment, you can care about it. This chapter is about choosing the best opportunities to get the stock sold off.

Look at Dividend Changes

Look for every situation where the valuation of the profits on the stock is beginning to decline. Study stock and company to see what triggers the transition. There might be serious problems inside the company, such as a lack of sales or court proceedings that trigger the valuation of the dividend to shift. And the slightest dividend reduction can be a source of alarm. A single decline may be a huge issue for your savings, with dividends worth pennies apiece. Losing one cent of a stock's 10,000 shares will result in a $100 reduction of the dividends. That, of course, is only one indication of what might happen.

Review Your Price Target

A successful buying approach is to stick with a defined price point. This can be the extent to which you like the stock to be independent of the form of trade you join. Start by looking at the expected returns per unit. A quarterly outlook for the next year will help you gain an insight into what's going on with a warehouse. This involves a study of how an organization generates its profits. This can help you define an estimated pace at which the stock will expand over time. See the earnings per share (EPS) forecast with caution. This is only a prediction of what will happen inside the company, depending on several variables. Clearly, you will have to use a stop-loss plan at this stage in case an organization failed to meet its estimate.

When the Volume Slows

The amount for your stock would have a major effect on your stock's progress. What happens when the demand begins to taper, and the stock isn't as common as it once was? The lack of volume may be an indication that your stock would not be going the same way you'd wanted it to go. A stock that had risen in value could display resistance as its amount diminishes. This means that consumers are not as willing to purchase a product as they used to be. Soon some people will start selling the stock. But you can sell your shares as quickly as possible, but that you can make sure you move out of a position until it becomes less enticing.

When a Business Is About to Go Bankrupt

When a business falls bankrupt, it can be catastrophic. There is a possibility that a company will arise better than ever out of the bankruptcy, such as what happened to numerous automotive firms in the U.S. A bankruptcy is more about making sure a corporation will reorganize itself to prevent a tough condition from getting worse.

The problems affecting a company may be too severe. A prime example of this is the discount store chain Toys R Us. The company moved through a period of closing stores in 2017 after it filed bankruptcy and then confirmed the second round of closures in 2018, leading the market presence of the brand to decline drastically. The major challenge is the bankruptcy will preclude a company from becoming sustainable and sustainable for investment. The stock's valuation would more than certainly collapse as a consequence of what is going on.

Signs of a Possible Bankruptcy

If you find that a stock is going to collapse in value with clear indicators of recession, so you can sell the stock. People will not experience damages because of an impending recession until it's too late, and the recession eventually occurs.

An organization is trying to slash its expenses but does not explain that it is doing so.

Many senior administrators or executives affiliated with a company might be quitting the company. If they realize the trouble is increasing and they want to get away before things get worse, they might quit early. They might also provide more comprehensive internal details on what's going on within the company, which allows it to fall apart.

Management may even be quiet and unable to share details on what is going on or whether such strategic decisions are being made.

Revenues fall dramatically and do not seem to display any indication of rebounding in their prices.

The cash balance statements may even disclose any important improvements. These involve improvements in how equipment maintenance plans can adjust and other routine efforts.

Tax Considerations for Losing Stocks

A large aspect of situations when the securities are losing value is they may provide you with a potential tax write-off. Any short-term losses you incur from stock purchases can outweigh short-term profits. When they drop value, you should sell your investments to better manage any taxes you'll have to pay. Particularly during the latter part of the year, you might do this if you have something that you've kept for a while, and you have to get rid of it. If you can lose revenue on the stock's disposal, you're at least going to hold your taxes off so high.

The short-term gains and losses would be registered separately from the long-term gains, the losses from a more mature portfolio that may be utilized by non-day traders before filing taxes. Check any of your holdings to decide if selling your shares is acceptable for your tax planning purposes at any particular period. For more guidance about what may be done to reduce your tax burden, please contact a local accountant or other tax planning specialist in your field.

Avoid Emotional Concerns

Moving a stock is often challenging, but moving anything you've had for a long period can be much tougher for you. You could feel that the stock that you had was something that you needed to hang on for as far as possible. You may have assumed that this will continue to increase in value. Perhaps it might also be the first stock you've ever traded-in.

You should still apply to your portfolio long-term stocks, but it doesn't suggest you can keep buying those stocks indefinitely. You have to disregard the emotional aspects of keeping a warehouse. You may be burdened with certain feelings when you try to hold your investments healthy.

How Much Money Should You Spend At One Time?

To get something out of day-trading is crucial to making enough funds for your stock trades. You should be conscious of how much you pay on a single transaction. It's real; you cannot pay more than you can manage on a single purchase. Is there some particular sum of money you can invest in each contract? There are no guidelines about how much expenditure an individual should be investing in. You ought to have a fair bit of common sense.

Here are a few suggestions:

Plan a Percentage Limit

Developing a percentage cap is the first method for handling capital through trades. That is the particular amount of the investments that you are going to use in a deal. The optimal percentage cap for your investments is 1 percent. If you have a balance of $25,000 for day trading, you can just be paying $250 per sale. That keeps your risk of trading too high. When the fund expands or shrinks in size, the 1 percent sum can always be utilized. If your portfolio winds up heading towards $26,000 in valuation, you can still use a $260 cap on a sale. You do have to stick to the 1 percent cap so you don't run the risk of wasting more than you can handle. Do not deviate from the norm except through your portfolio shrinks.

Review the Cents Per Risk

The second technique to use includes calculating the cents by chance. This is a calculation of the difference in cents between your stock entry point and the stop command you apply to it. If a cents per risk ratio was too big, you would choose to spend less capital on a project.

If the value is a little similar to the original price, you will have more.

How Big of a Position Should You Have?

Holding a target of 1 percent for your transactions is important, so you can think of how many securities you purchase at a time. This quick equation can be used to get an understanding of how large the place should be:

1. Take the entire sum of capital you'll be placing at risk.

2. Divide location by danger by cents. (In decimal terms this would be; 50 would be 0.5.)

3. You can know the total amount of securities you will be buying.

Let's presume you're going to be spending $250 in a portfolio despite getting 50 cents to stop order. You'd divide by 0.5 $250, which is equivalent to 500. That is, you can acquire up to 500 shares at once. Be mindful of potential transaction payments related to the portfolio contracts. Although this does not cost as much as the whole transaction itself, it also pays to recognize at least the charges while preparing the trading strategy.

On a note similar to this, there can be occasions that you need to round out the request. You do not have the opportunity to sell 250 or 270 stocks. Instead, you can be asked by a broker to exchange 200 or 300 securities. You'd have to round the amount up or down, but for an even sum, the dealer would have a simpler time to conduct the deal. You have the option, but if necessary, it is better to select the lower number. Use the 200 share option for this example. This would obviously be less than 1 percent of your overall assets, so at this juncture, that's perfect. You also need to spend wisely in the stock so you can finally step ahead and improve your position later on. The smaller order is going to be less of danger, but that's another matter.

A Sense of Balance

You need to keep the finances in check. Putting so much capital into a stock could result in you spending more money than you can manage. There's still a risk a project fails. The last option you might do is to drastically shrink your investments to where you can't afford a reasonable investment anymore.

You can't afford to actually make inexpensive trades all the time, though. You ought to invest a reasonable sum of money in your company if you wish to make anything substantial out of your company. Anyone who invests less would definitely not be reaping the rewards of becoming a good day trader.

How Are Preferred Shares Different from Common Shares?

On the surface, it seems that preferred stock securities are identical to common shares. It reflects one's ownership of a company. The stock price is often focused on the roles of earning and selling. Preferred stock shares can have the same value as common stockholders or are similar to the value at least.

Preferred shares send you dividends that are settled upon at the point of a deal, whereas dividends that differ in value depending on profits and other things are paid out by common share. For a preferred share, you'll recognize the size of the dividend per year. In particular, the dividend may be considerably higher than a common share dividend. Nevertheless, a preferred share would not grant you are voting privileges in the relations of the business, such as the sale of common stock. That would not actually be a concern when you understand the value of the preferred stock.

What About Maturity?

A significant aspect of dealing with common stock securities is how long you get to hang onto the stock. When the preferred stock hits maturity, you get the initial investment back plus any dividends on it returned. This is a good idea, but it will take a while to hit maturity with the preferred stock. For it to happen, you'd have to wait around 30 to 40 years. Obviously, with day-trading in mind, that's not something you can do. For anything, that will only be offering you a daily source of income that you can use to invest in the future. This is advantageous in that even though the preferred stock sinks to zero, you can always get the maximum valuation of the portfolio. At maturity, the entire amount would be paid out, thereby granting you maximum coverage for the existence of the product. It's a lot different from the common stock because if the stock really dropped to nothing, you will get none.

Why Would a Business Issue Preferred Shares?

A corporation will sell common stock certificates to investors as a way to collect funds for business activities. This occurs when a company has sold common stocks and bonds on a daily basis. However, usually, companies delay until they have sold common stocks and shares since they are not since difficult to sell as the preferred stock. A business may terminate the dividends on preferred shares. This doesn't happen very much, so there's still an opening. In reality, it is feasible for a corporation to do this and not to fear being sued for default. This is separate from loans where a corporation will default if the debt in such assets cannot be paid off.

A corporation will also benefit from preferred stock tax incentives. A business would not be expected to pay taxes on any of the funds it collects for the stock. Growing the overall sum of capital it won't have to pay back is better for a company because it doesn't take a long time to get preferred stock released on the market.

The firm would compensate investors' interest depending on how the stock does. Fortunately, this benefit would not be liable to taxation for the company. A large amount of the tax load is thus lifted entirely. Be told that the business selling the stock would not benefit from such tax advantages.

Important Concerns

You have to be careful, as tempting as is the chosen product. You could begin by looking at the interest rates correlated with preferred stock. Try to purchase the stock at a cheaper cost, as profits would have a greater opportunity to rise with time. Something that has a high cost is most likely to receive smaller overtime payouts. Moreover, rising interest rates trigger increases in returns on other stock-related assets. That cuts into the dividend gains you'd make.

You have to be very vigilant of how, with time, the common stock aligned with a preferred stock varies. The dilemma is that as stock values go up, the corporation that sold them will cash in common stock securities. You would also lose the valuation really going up on the preferred shares. You could earn compensation on any shares you lost, but even though the compensation will not come similar to what you'd get if the shares matured.

Will These Strategies Work For Other Types of Investments?

All the points in this document you've read about are planned with stock trades or options in mind. For any other project, you may be involved in, you may suggest partnering with certain techniques. The amazing thing in the business environment today is that consumers have plenty of various opportunities to participate in. People will transact stocks and options as well as securities, mutual funds, and more. Cryptocurrencies can also be used in today's sector.

Don't believe the techniques you've read about here would fit with all investing forms. The concern for so many of today's equity assets is that they all have multiple factors that may directly affect their beliefs. Commodities, for example, are also influenced by geographical factors and patterns on what customers would want or what companies might use. Mutual funds are also distinctive in terms of how they offer professionally designed solutions assembled by experts to their investors' benefit. There are Cryptocurrencies all over the location. In reality, the products you invest in differ from one sector to another. For example, the energy industry is distinct from the retail or hospitality industries. Different variables can significantly affect the manner in which patterns grow and how market prices may differ.

Such assets outside the stocks are often expected to wind up dealing with the same patterns and metrics as stocks. The Doji can predominate on a foreign currency pair. A pennant, cup, and handle or some other pattern of exchange may appear on a merchandise transaction. In order to obtain details about certain specific projects, you will also have to deal with several key principles. The issue with non-stock investments is that they are very drastic and complex in the variables which affect them.

Overall, if you plan to use the points you have gained regarding other forms of investments in this text, you should be exceedingly cautious. If you do, you can still use them, but that doesn't guarantee they would work.

Chapter 11: Links and Steps to Activate with a Broker

Investing profitably enables you to use the same broker company that conforms with your financial priorities, training qualifications, and personal style. Choosing the right online financial manager that fits your requirements, particularly for new shareholders, may make a big difference with an interesting new investment portfolio and severe loss.

Although there are no entirely convinced-fire means of guaranteeing returns on investment, there is indeed a way of setting oneself help and protect by choosing the investment account that better fits your description. In this tutorial, we'll dissolve anything that you can search for in your perfect broker, of the apparent to something not-so-accurate (as how simple it really is to get help from a real person when you really need it).

Key Points

- Exposure to the markets is cheap and easy due to a number of retail brokers operating online portals.

- Various online traders are tailored for a particular category of the customer – from lengthy-term buy-or-hold newcomers to professional, successful day trades.

- Picking the right broker online needs any proper research to have the best out of your investment. Obey the measures and recommendations to pick the right one in this post.

1: Remind Yourself About Your Desires

Take a minute to zero in on what is really essential to you that in a trading site, before they start pressing on broker advertising. Based on the financial goals and also where people are along the investing learning process, the solution may be subtly different.

When you're just heading out, features such as simple educational tools, detailed glossaries, fast access to help personnel, and the opportunity to learn trades until you actually play with actual money might be priorities.

If you already have certain investing expertise into your belt but are ready to get ambitious, you may like more strong-level information or interpretation-based tools published by active traders and experts and a broad range of simple and technical info.

A genuinely professional trader, maybe someone who has already carried out dozens of trades but also looking for a different broker, would offer preference to sophisticated charting tools, dependent order rights, and the right to trade futures, bonds, shares, and specified-income instruments, and stocks.

Be frank on what you see on the investing path right now, where you'd like to go. Would you try to create an IRA and 401(k) retirement plan and concentrate on passive assets that will produce tax-free money? Would you like to look down your nose in day-trading and don't know how to get started? Would you prefer the thought of designing your entire portfolio and tailoring it, or are you able to hire a specialist to make sure it's done right?

Relying on the direction you follow, there could be even more queries that you may need to address when you acquire knowledge and develop your objectives. Beginning with any of these four key criteria for now, though, will help you decide which one of the broker's features we will cover below would be most relevant. We also provided some test questions below each wider subject to help keep the analytical impulses flowing:

1. You're an aggressive or inactive investor in general? Want to be very hands-on to do day- and swing-trades? Can you finally see yourself abandoning the 9-to-5 routine and being a maximum-time entrepreneur? Or, then, are you searching for a few good assets with little to no day-to-day contact to carry for the longer term?

2. How many do you understand? Which sort of trades do you like to carry out? Will you be the sort of shareholder that understands what they like to do and only wants a forum that allows trading simple and fast, or would you like the broker with such a broader arsenal of tools to help you look for chances? Which kind of stocks are you targeting? Stocks, ETFs, mutual funds? Would you want to exchange stocks, derivatives, or fixed-income instruments even if you're more sophisticated? What are retailing margins? Want exposure to contingent orders, longer trading hours, and currency trading choices?

3. Want to help? What type? Would you go towards the DIY road, learn how to view charts or financial details in order to discover and carry out your own trading, or would you like to employ a pro? How are you in the learning process because you decide to go for it yourself? Which kind of tools are you supposed to use to draw on your understanding? Need quick access to help workers, or will you discover what you have to know via online learning resources? Would

you want to conduct trades remotely, or do you like to dial in and get a broker and support you with a procedure?

4. What are the targets? In what do you invest? Why do you choose for an investment? Seek to supplement your daily salary to boost your existing living standards? Was there some special case or cost you'd like to fund? Would you plan to potentially be your main source of revenue for this? Are you seeking to set up private pensions, and if so, do you still want a retirement plan, or would you like to start a new one through your fund of choice?

Such queries are not replied incorrectly. Be honest about how many of your important movements, energy, and struggle you are willing to put in the investments. Over time, your answers will shift, and that is good. Will not try to predict any of your desires and priorities for the remainder of your career. Just start right now, with what you have right now.

2: Narrow Down Your Area

Now that you're having a clear understanding of what their investment objective is or what essential services you are going to start looking for in your perfect brokers, it is time to winnow down your choices a little bit. Although there are many brokerage elements that might be more essential to some shareholders than others, there are also some things that should have any reliable brokerage online. Checking the simple needs for such a wide variety of choices is a perfect way to easily narrow the spectrum.

Stock Broker and Trust Regulation

Is the courier a Financial Investor Security Company (SIPC) member? Usually, there should be a form of description or warning at the end of the homepage. The company can be easily looked up on the SIPC platform.

Is the broker a part of the regulatory body for the financial sector (FINRA)? It should be noted very clearly in a location that is easy to find. You can view brokerages on the website of FINRA's Brokerage Check.

Is the company protected by the National Federal insurance Company (FDIC) as it sells checking or investment accounts, or all other investment items? Investment plans - such as securities or mutual funds invested in commodities, shares, futures, and insurance policies - are not covered by FDIC, since the security of the assets cannot be assured. Moreover, if the company sells CDs, Term deposit Arrangements (MMDAs), banking accounts, or investment accounts, the FDIC will completely back them up.

What form of protection do they have to cover you in the event that the business fails? As a participant of a SIPC, the business will provide policies with a cap of at minimum $500,000 per client, with $250,000 reserved for cash complaints. If the corporation conforms to the consumer rights Rule, further coverage should also be provided over and above the SIPC's minimum standards.

Is there some sort of protection against fraud? Does the business compensate you for fraud-related losses? Be sure that you double test what the company expects of you will be reimbursed. Figure out whether you need to have some evidence or take clear measures for your own safety.

What is it the new consumers assume? Start looking for brokerage user feedback online, utilizing terms such as "insurance allegation," "fraud defense," and "customer care." Obviously, online comments can usually be viewed with a pinch of salt - certain people feel like moaning. Moreover, when there are many users from various places that are all voicing the same claim, then you might want to further examine.

Online Monitoring and Account Safety

It's crucial to know well how your data is secured by a brokerage.

Does it provide two-factor protection on the broker website? Can you get the choice in response to your key to triggering a protection feature? Responding to security requests, obtaining special, moment-sensitive keys through email or text, or utilizing data security keys that fit in your USB, may be popular.

Which kind of software is the broker employing to keep the data secure? Find out how the broker utilizes "cookies" or cryptography and how that explicitly describes how it utilizes them to secure the account details and how it functions.

Will be the company still marketing details regarding consumers to third parties, including advertising companies? The response, of course, should be no.

Brokers Trading Deals

Since the sorts of methods, you will rely on your objectives; the following elements should also be checked quickly to weed out investment banks that will simply not make your life easier.

Besides regular (taxable) mutual funds, what sorts of funds does a broker offer? If you already have investment income, for example, find out how you should open a health savings Arrangement (ESA) or a correctional account for the child or even other members.

Can you access a bank account? See if the broker has Roth or alternative savings plans and whether you should carry over an unused 401 K and IRA.

There are different companies for various targets for investment? For example, find out how the broker has handled accounts on offer. Often, find out which various forms of portfolios have investment requirements.

Can you use the Brokerage to manage employee retirement funds? This can apply if you are a proprietor of a business. These Account forms include Basic or SEP IRAs.

Would the fund have alternatives for Self-Directed retirement funds or the Single 401 K? What happens if you are the only team member in your small company.

3: Calculate the Charges

Although there could be some items more relevant for you other than payments, you could begin with a fairly good picture of how many you could spend to use some specific brokers.

For others, whether the product provides functionality that it lacks affordable rivals, a low prime might be acceptable. In fact, though, at valuation costs and selling profits, you ought to risk as necessary of the interest earned as necessary.

Beginning from the end result, you can quickly decide that stock traders have become too costly to accept and are not really suited to the type of investing operation you're focusing on.

Brokers Account Income

Will the broker make a fee for the account opening?

Is there a Total Deposit? Please remember that investment funds have a minimum investment of $1,000 and sometimes more than that, but that isn't relevant as a financial institution that requires you to deposit the lowest possible amount of money only to open the account.

Are there really any maintenance charges per annum or yearly account? If so, were they forgiven for bigger accounts, or can they be skipped effectively even though your checking account is low? For instance, if the holders concur to collect documentation digitally, Vanguard renounces its yearly fee.

Was the dealer providing equal entry to a trade site as a result of their membership? The online platform will ideally match your needs if you are just beginning out.

There is a Pay-to-Play trading site Pro and Advanced? When you're a very seasoned user, it's crucial to learn whether or maybe not you should have to pay to update your profile or get to the speed-up software and services. For buyers who choose to position a certain amount of trades each year or spend a certain sum, certain specialized systems are safe.

What are those margin prices? Margin investing is for really professional customers only, who recognize the dangers. If you're a value player, the statement is not going to relate to you.

What is the total amount of loan and balance of the account? For greater quantities, most investment banks will give lower rates, so don't let that be a reason for the client to borrow more than they should.

Commissions for Trading

Will exchange commissions rely on whether you have spent or how many you move through brokerage? Vanguard's trading fees, for instance, vary according to the size of the account, whilst also E*TRADE provides a lowered council to clients who buy and sell greater than 30 times a quarter.

William Schwab's fees are smaller than rivals; however, to create an account, you will spend nearly $1,000. Think you should look at the rates that are most applicable to you, depending on your expected balance of account and trade activity.

Will common fee rates extend to information visualization? If you prepare more than stock trading, make sure that you know whatever the fees are for trading options, securities, futures, and perhaps other bonds.

If you think for investment funds or ETFs, will there be payment-free choices? What's really the least investment? Be sure that investments that allow you to purchase and sell for cheap do not charge certain forms of fees anyway. Investments often came with various types of expenses, all of which can pounce on you. Check the proposal of every investment you are contemplating to make sure you grasp all the risks involved.

Will the company makes any free or discounted transactions? The number of 'bonus' trades you earn may vary based on your outstanding balance, so be sure you double-check what's being offered for the level of your account that would apply. Often, make sure to test what sorts of transactions apply for the reduced price – whether it's just for shares and whether it includes ETFs, futures, or specific-income securities.

Is the contract timetable favorable to the sort of trading that you can do? Are you compensated with more successful trading, or are you penalized? For example, prices for Vanguard are increasing from the first twenty-five trades for Specification and Main competitor clients, or after 100 transactions for Flagship Enable clients, as you see in the above chart. This means consumers focused on active, purchase-and-hold investments get the most value.

Conversely, for the first 30 transactions of every given fifth, E*TRADE provides discounted fees, and committed participants are paid most frequently by utilizing the site.

When the dealer offers consulting services, how many do they charge? Is there a certain balance of account required to pay for such services? When, for whatsoever the reason, you are not trying to run your own investments, make sure to pay really great consideration to advisor costs.

4: Check the Broker Network

Although every brokerage will provide a reasonably clear overview of all sorts of applications and services a trading broker provides, often giving it a quick drive is the only way to determine the consistency of the product. With brokers who require you to set up an account for free, the initiative to go through the sign-up phase might also be worthwhile only to reach the payment system if this is what's required.

If the company provides a web-based portal that can be used by anybody or a free online application needing no-string sign-up, do whatever you can to use the software that you can really need free.

Unless you're a more experienced investor, and there's no easy way to mess around in front of "Pro" software, you could get a decent understanding of a standard of the products from a brokerage only by gazing through the simple collection. Unless there is little that appears appealing in the basic model, it's doubtful that the advanced form would be value the trouble either.

But from the other side of their free services, some firms offer a vast array of gadgets and information, so just don't start writing off brokerage firms with just one platform.

We've also invested a fair deal of time shortening the options based on quality and simple account deals. Now that we have finally got to the fun part, make sure to consume days reading also at features in various areas available.

Go into the steps for putting a transaction to see if the mechanism runs smoothly. Take several stock quotations and other stocks, then press on each tab to look at what sort of data the website offers. Additionally, you can search out any scanners or other resources available to help you identify funds that follow clear requirements.

Answer to the questions Whilst checking platforms:

What kinds of assets on the system may you trade? You would have already governed out any systems that do not enable you to exchange the bonds that interest you. Make sure this website helps you to transact preferred stock, IPOs, stocks, futures, and a fixed amount of income securities automatically. If you do not see clear protections on the website, but you realize it's sponsored by the company, seek to look at your settings or perform a fast check and see if you can trigger certain apps to read about authorization criteria.

Are real-time quotes? Do they flow? There are many places you could get a price estimate for just a given location, although not every one of them can have the latest up-to-date detail. Be sure you know in which you can find streaming knowledge in real-time to ensure the trades are timely. For instance, Vanguard's web-based system provides quick-time data on its countdown clock personal profiles but requires refreshing manuals. Easy results at the quote stage were postponed by 10 min more than that. Schwab's electronic quotes often entail downloading guides, but all provide real-time viewing data across the free Street-smart Edge app and its cloud-enabled equivalent.

Can you create your own custom watch lists or alerts? If you are trying to be more of an affiliate marketer, in relation to email, you will probably like being able to get alerts via text and make different watch lists various criteria.

Do the framework supply inspectors, which you can personalize to discover inventories, ETFs, index funds, or any other bonds that fulfill your special requirements? Even if you're new and don't know what all of the choices literally mean, play with the different variables to have a concept of how easy to use the tools. A strong interface should be designed conceptually and simple to use.

What sorts of commissions can you put? Go into the movements for placing the trade, as well as look at what kinds of requests are being offered. A basic system should normally offer market limits, restrict, hold back, and stop boundaries. A better framework will also enable you to put chasing keep orders or consumer-on-close instructions.

If you're searching to do comparatively several transactions, and you're not concerned in a day- and swing-trading, there should be a basic choice of order types. However, if you're trying to look to get out of trading stocks gritty-gritty, you must look for just a wider choice. If you are more experienced, you will look for just the option to position contractual instructions that enable you can set up several transactions with different triggers, which will immediately execute when the requirements you define are met.

Do you really have access to the timing of orders and the implementation of trades? At least one simple platform will allow you to position good-for-day trades (meaning they could be performed at any time during working hours) or nice-until-canceled trades.

A more sophisticated platform allows you to position boundary orders with more variation, like put-or-kill (which cancels its order immediately if it is not filled out immediately) and Instantaneous or terminate (which cancels its order immediately if it is not filled in at least in part immediately).

Will you deal in Long Hrs.? Stock or ETF transactions arise during regular 9:30 a.m. business hours. - 16 P.M. Ap, the times of pre-market and post-hours. Each brokerage will have its own description of the different time periods covered by such extra hour sessions. For e.g., Schwab has post-shipment trade starting at 8:00 a.m., while E*TRADE's pre-market sessions begin around 7 a.m.

Not all systems begin trading over extra periods, and some allow only after-hours trading, not during premarket hours. You can be paid a premium for longer trading hours; just be sure that you check the conditions of certain transactions and ensure that you are not caught by surprise.

Again, that feature might not be all that good for modern investors. However, checking the extra hours trading strategy of a brokerage is important for more experienced traders or others who are trying to be very involved.

Charting Characteristics

Now that you've been messing with the application a little more, take a closer look at a charting feature to test the options available for you. Listen to what sorts of data it can map, how simple it is to move among charting studies and analyzing common or industry results, and how you should modify and save to later use.

What chart patterns are on a chart? Generally, the stronger, the more. So, at the least, higher times such as quantity, RSI, exponential moving avg, swing trading, MACD, as well as stochastics should be plottable. If one of those key guidelines is missing, it's time to move forward. Basically, a few business events, such as quarterly results, stock divides, and dividends, must also be plottable.

The following are instances of two distinct technological menus. These are less than the optimal alternative. Note that volume is not plottable:

It also has an impressive technological choice, which involves several choices for each form of indicator. It also lets you map the basic data and also has a search feature:

Could you use the same map to compare various stocks or indices?

Can you draw trends, free-form graphs, Prime numbers circles, or arcs, or any other markings on the chart?

Does the website have a trade publication or any other way to save your work? If you're going to speak charts or you're a seasoned investor making notes to keep track of yourself, finding a way to design and archive your graphs is a very useful resource. Things linked include:

• Aside from building historical trends, should you easily draw on the map to illustrate key things, so you can recall when to check later?

• Can you store the maps once you have adjusted them to your needs?

• May you make information for use later?

• Would you place certain comments on the table and make sure you recognize what they refer to when you glance at them later?

Some Other Options

Please note that many of these choices can be accessed only on a Professional or Advanced device. If you're a successful, experienced investor, you'll definitely want to have a brokerage that provides all those options. Whether you're a more casual investor or simply don't want to spend a fee for bells or whistles that you're not ready to, keeping to a standard free platform is perfect.

• Can you simplify trades with custom rules or with manufactured methodologies?

• Can the network be tailored to acknowledge specific price, indicator, and modulation diagram patterns?

• Can you set alerts to inform you when a contrasting pattern is found on the device?

Is the site or forum allowed to export paper? For shareholders, paper trade is a place to practice putting or performing transactions without even utilizing capital. It is a perfect place to train potential successful investors and investors with all levels of expertise to try out innovative ideas and refine their abilities without causing losses.

Is back testing enabled on the model? Back testing helps you to replicate a transaction based on the past results of your preferred defense, another method to check techniques to get familiar with the method before placing cash on a line. It's a way to put a retroactive, hypothetical transaction and then see what might have changed if you actually carried that out in actual life.

5: How Well is the Stockbroker Teach its Customers?

While a reliable and efficient payment system is important, you should take a moment to discover educational deals from the brokerage and check out another search feature.

You ought to be capable of locating for words you don't recognize or to get guidance about how to view data because you are a value player. If there is a topic you have been beginning to wonder about and a measurement you do not fully comprehend, do a test run using the search feature and see what you can efficiently find the info you really want.

Know, for one developer, what is elegant or eco-friendly can be a terrifying maze with meaningless web searches for the next, so it's essential to choose a tool that you can operate with.

If you've been navigating a site for about 20 minutes, you will be able to ask the following issues fairly quickly. If you can't, and a fast check for clear answers from the web doesn't deliver the details you need, it's usually an indication that the trading system isn't for you.

Quality and Accessibility of stockbrokers

All of the world's educational services are worthless because you can't conveniently reach them. A strong forum or website will also give a wide variety of learning resources in different formats to ensure that consumers access the content they need efficiently and conveniently in a way that fits with their preferred style. Once we delve into the different categories of educational institutions that you can anticipate from a successful brokerage, make sure that such tools were user-friendly first.

What kinds of education programs do the financial adviser offer? The layout needs to start working for you, whether it provides video clips, podcasts, podcasts, or written books.

Where does the information originate from? If the trader syndicates from other pages, guarantee all certain pages are trustworthy. If the platform features a forum or other material by readers, then please ensure that the posting writers have expertise and knowledge, which you can believe.

How easy or intuitive is navigation to the site and platform? Make sure that going to the Selling screen from a study page is a quick operation. You do not want to look like walking around in loops. Make sure the various topics on the site are easy to find.

Does broker sell resources for beginners? This might involve pronunciation guides or how-to papers, basic analyzes, diversification of investments, how to view scientific studies, and other topics for beginners.

How successful is the search feature on the platform? By typing into a common investment term or looking for subjects you have queries about, you can find this out. How quickly has the search feature been able to get the details that you needed? Is this knowledge available automatically, or do you need to scroll on a few sites to get through?

Here's an instance of a non-user-friendly search function:

Although Vanguard lets you use its tracking tool to map the relative power index (RSI), its search feature does not seem to know the expression.

Resources Monitoring

Is there enough review with respect to will security? Which will provide multi-source analyst scores, real-time stories, and the market as well as sector details relevant.

Is there any of the essential data accessible? For starters, stock portfolios will contain the issuance company's historical records, such as annual releases, financial results (like working capital, operating statement and statement of cash), dividend distributions, trading volume and repurchases, and SEC disclosures. Any insider-trading operation must also be warned.

Are business details open for U.S. and global markets? How regarding information from manufacturing and from the sector? How thoroughly can you immerse yourself in the big picture circumstances affecting business performance?

6: Ease of Depositing and Withdrawing Funds

Is there enough review with respect to will security? Which will provide multi-source analyst scores, real-time stories, and the market as well as sector details relevant.

Is there any of the essential data accessible? For starters, stock portfolios will contain the issuance company's historical records, such as annual releases, financial results (like working capital, operating statement and statement of cash), dividend distributions, trading volume and repurchases, and SEC disclosures. Any insider-trading operation must also be warned.

Are business details open for U.S. and global markets? How regarding information from manufacturing and from the sector? How thoroughly can you immerse yourself in the big picture circumstances affecting business performance?

Removing Funds

How long would it take to recover the funds from selling the investments? Making sure you test the unified group with the numerous forms of shares that you are trying to sell.

What are income payments or tax payments? How quickly are those assets available to invest? For retiring?

How convenient is using the investment account to remove funds? Figure out how you can transfer through ACH wire, wire, or email and also how far it would take to get into your banking account for all those funds. Also find out if there are any withdrawal fees.

Will the broker offer the option of adding a debit and ATM card to your credit card? It is often given for a mutual fund, as well as other times to use this service; you have to open a connected checking and saving account. Find out what other ATMs you can use if you have a card option, so there are some costs involved with using the card.

7: Support to Customers

By now, you've already limited your choices to one of two brokerage firms that actually blow you up in terms of money, functionality, and functionality. If you've reached the dream forum, or are already on the board, just take a couple more minutes to search a brokerage aid section you're contemplating.

When you're a potential user and feel stressed, make absolutely sure you can rapidly and effectively get in contact with the military members. When you're technologically inept, try to ensure your tech support department is easy to get in contact with and accessible 24/7.

Although these things won't make and break a brokerage choice, it's always important to know you recognize where and where to get support.

- Is there a designated amount where you should call a person asking for trade aid?

- Ensure you are informed of any potential phone-assisted trading costs.

- Can you call an automatic number for the simple queries?

- Ultimate support what? And what were the Assistance ask-in hours?

- What are the operating hours for telephone lines? Will you dial 24/7, or do the phones only work outside office hours?

- There is an email for those that are opposed to contacting that you use to get timely support?

- Does the company use a safe network for internal transmission of relevant documentation and client questions?

- Maybe you are having a normal issue but don't want to annoy the member? Is there a viewable FAQ segment that responds to a large range of perspectives?

- How for tech backing? Are there specific phone lines, telephone numbers, or chat networks to access professional support?

8: Go and Take Next Moves

Whatever broker has by far the most active campaign, we realize it can be enticing to sign up for. However, good investing takes dedication to details far before you position your first order.

If you're planning to take trading a lengthy-term hobby, a long-term career, or even a way to boost your pension fund, then it's important to use the resources and tools that will help you deal for an enjoyable and successful experience.

Hopefully, by adopting an in-depth tutorial you've found the forum that would better fit your requirements, which they may be. On our stockbroker rating page, you will find support filtering via the various brokers.

Chapter 12: Common Strategies to Follow

We're going to speak about some of the more popular tactics that certain people may have learned about, even though they're not particularly acquainted with the equity market's workings.

Buying On Down Days

In general, that is not a terrible thing. The broker calls you up and advises you that there appears to be a down day on the street, and it may be a smart opportunity to pick up any stocks at the low.

As you'll have come to know, when it comes to capital market activity there are still two sides of a coin.

If you're someone with a strong market analysis system that focused your investment decisions on sound facts and numbers, then a down day might potentially be a moment when you might want to pick up any stocks you've purchased at a lower price. Also, a down day doesn't imply you're wasting any of your money on those better cost products. The astute investor will drive the positions in sections more frequently than not, with the expectation that a down day might quite well turn out to be a down week. That will indicate decent rates for products picking up.

However, if you are merely betting on the tips and calls of the broker, a splurge into the market on a down-day could become a cause for depression if the market doldrums continue over the week or even a month. You just purchased it, you figured it was a decent deal, and now it's gone down much more.

Buying on down days cannot be seen as a tactic alone but as part of a well-planned framework as a whole. There is, nevertheless, a claim that purchasing on down days may be a tactic too, and here is how it goes.

You buy on a day off. If the price drops more down the next day, you pay exactly what you paid. Then if the price drops more down the following day, you repeat the prior day's sales again. You'd only made seven multiples of the original first-day purchase at this point.

You then pursue this buy if the downward go on before there is a rebound that the market price does not fall below the day before, and so you sell it all off.

Since you've acquired product in higher numbers at cheaper rates, you've basically downgraded the expenses, and thus, when there's a market spike, selling off anything can be a benefit net.

The difficulty with this is the requirement to provide large quantities of money to continue the endless purchasing. Imagine something occurring for 15 days, how many multiples will it have been? Not something I'd suggest, so it's not worth the risk-benefit ratio to me.

Dollar-Cost Averaging

This is because many investment analysts and citizens are moving the shares and exchange-traded securities (ETFs)

Are you really trying? The basic principle is that you designate a date, claim the first day of the month to dive into the financial instruments in your currency, regardless of the market fluctuations that day. You're here.

Then do this regularly over the following months, with the period chosen over putting the capital into investing per the first day of the month.

You basically take out of scenario the timing of the market or actually randomize the timing of the market. By adding funds per month on a particular day in the period, you neglect the market dynamics at that moment of time in merely concentrate on reaching your roles.

Financial analysts prefer this concept because it makes the assets of the clientele easy to handle. Of note, the dollar cost measure, under such circumstances, still has its merits. It is our job to know what these requirements are and how the overall cost of the dollar can be exploited for our gain.

Generally speaking, when the economy is a rising trend, getting a set sum to spend on a given date would mean that you are only buying fewer units at a better price.

The same would be valid when the demand is downward heading, where the set volume will then cause a greater buying quantity at a lower price.

The average cost to most folk would be the commercial appeal of the dollar, the fact that it looks like an idiot-proof way to invest. Think about it; you're setting aside a comfortable sum per month or annum, or whatever period you choose. Then you literally plunge it into the stock or stocks that you have picked. More frequently than not, though, you will drive that into mutual funds or exchange-traded funds since they are, in reality, investments that are investing in various securities and properties, and so you believe that might be best for liquidity and stability.

For me, whether you intend to participate in the equity market and its relevant capital services, time should never be removed from the table entirely. Why? Why?

People, who happily have dollars in an average of one year or even two to three years, can lose half or a ton of their financial value just because they choose to participate in a bear market because their predominant plan was to go long or buy stock.

If one truly decided to sell or invest like an ostrich, so at least seven to fourteen years would need to be the minimum horizon. This is such that you can view yourself in two simultaneous economic cycles and thereby have a subsequent effect on the capital markets.

To me, the average cost of the dollar has its benefits, but you need to understand how to do it and, most specifically, to determine if it is really acceptable for your specific do. This sort of investing plan will be perfect for people who have limitless stamina, have a decent career or extra cash flow every month rolling in, and don't even get concerned by the sums they're plugging into the markets. The crux of the matter is that they can spend a sum they feel really happy with and that they would rarely not have to change the level of money even in the direst emergencies.

These people would profit from this approach because it suits them fairly well because they actually don't have a crippling curiosity even on a weekly basis in researching the financial markets. While their earnings are good, they would find it exceedingly challenging to overtake timers in the sector. I tell this honestly and based on what I heard and learned. It does not knock on the cost balancing technique of the dollar at all.

Like I said earlier, there are numerous roads leading to Rome, and everyone has their favorite route.

Indeed, the overall expense of the dollar may be perceived as a stand-alone tactic, albeit a very simplified one. However, those who wish to reap full profits from it will need to monitor and timing the sector, and others who only want to make their capital function better for them without suffering through problems would also need to consider a longer keeping duration or horizon.

Bear Market Strategy

This is basically a purchase on bad days' situation derivation. Generally, bear markets are known as such after the economy has experienced a drop of twenty percent in stock prices or where the stocks have been exposed to sustain downward pressure for several months or even years.

For me, bear markets can have numerous and varying mathematical metrics to decide by, so a rather easy approach is to head out into the streets and start talking to people you're accustomed to seeing on a regular basis. Taxi drivers, restaurant waiters, and maybe also primary school instructors! If neither of them would like to chat with you about the equity market, you're potentially in the money if you put your bet that the economy is definitely in the doldrums and the sector is somewhat bearish.

Everyone becomes a financial market whiz when the shares are optimistic, and that is where the word irrational exuberance introduces itself. By comparison, when no one tries to give their well-meaning suggestions about which stocks to buy or sell, and when even the stock market whisper will bring people into jitters or advise them to keep away, then you definitely realize that the bear market is on its way.

The solution for the bear market is also fairly basic. Simply define the bear market era accurately, and

What you do need now, though, is trust. And when other people are huddled at home with their cash fund collections, you'll head out into the street to purchase products.

Creating your confidence would require a clear and strong study of the firms that are piquing your attention, but still ensuring that you do not overestimate yourself in the department of capital. Sell markets may be reasonably brief, although others can be reasonably deep, which is why the confidence of remaining engaged is necessary to understand the opportunity for benefit.

These sorts of scenarios do not exist on a regular or weekly basis, but it would be fair to assume that those concerned with day trading or short-term swing trading wouldn't have anything to do here. The bear market plan is really about people who normally have cash on hand, because they've done their homework in such a way that when the moment arrives they're beyond doubt and can behave in trust when they're backed up by anyone else.

One quirk is that others would also mix the method of cost averaging the currency with this tactic for the bear market. This involves foresight and confidence that the bear market is still on us, and then a clear scheme can be formulated to trigger regular stock and fund sales while the markets begin to fall. Some prefer this as opposed to trying to plunge in larger amounts in one go, while some tend to hold to their calculations and focus their investments on price ranges that they have determined to be of worth.

Again I would claim in both situations, there is no right or wrong. Most notably, a reasonable match for the customer needs to be the approach. As I would like to suggest, if you earn a hundred thousand dollars but are continuously shivering with anxiety and sweat-drenched, I would rather take advantage of ten thousand to sleep comfortably and without any worries.

The bear market strategy has its position and period for usage, but due to the very existence of being a bear market, it is not ideal for those searching for fast trades. It's a really nice way for me to spend the surplus funds for which you have no need and to sit invested in securities or instruments that can't earn profits for a few years down the line.

Day Trading

This used to be a fad because I was already battling the market. At this point in time, I believe it to always be. Many day-trading advocates will claim it's one of the easiest ways to sell and get wealthy. In the afternoon you reach and leave both of your places. You scout your stocks and plan them throughout the day. Within the trading time period, you make all your choices, and so after the market ends, you are a happier individual, and you will go to bed with no fears, unlike others that have current securities.

All this is well and dandy, but as I have already said, there will always be two sides to everything with respect to the stock market.

If you lock yourself up and only be willing to exchange within the time span of a day, what happens if you don't have any decent trades to pick from? Do you believe you'd have the opportunity to indulge in a transaction, or you would not really gain money for the day? What occurs if the condition of this sort of exchange is less than one day, two days, or even three days in a row? Could you guess how much tension and anxiety the day trader has to endure at this juncture? The day trader may therefore be compelled to participate in a deal that may not be the most desirable to get out of this. That represents an enhanced loss risk.

The typical counter-argument to this will be that the world of stocks, as well as financial instruments, is so large that at least one decent trade would certainly be set up every day. The world may be large, but your resources will restrict the degree to which you would comfortably evaluate the stocks you choose to sell. There is just so much that artificial intelligence and computerized aids will achieve, with the human brain also required for deeper research.

The other part of day trading where you have to remember will be on the benefit side. Tell you sold a portfolio for the day. Twenty points in the day went up, and you've happily banked with the income. It holes out the following day, when the market exchange only opens at a far higher price than the closing price of the previous day. This kind of scenario occurs when there are good reports from overnight or when the purchasing desire is too strong.

As a day trader, anytime some kind of upward sprint occurs, you are pushed into the periphery. You may be able to fall into the act and just leap through the structures and laws, and that will be the first move to foolishness.

Day trading is almost of an opportunistic practice to me. If there is an optimal time to do so, we can do it. It's really much about how they used to do hunting and fishing - in seasons. When the season is perfect for day trading, we can do so because it really does increase your sharpness and contribute to your benefit capacity. We should have our other structures and strategies to focus on when the season isn't there. Trading on the day doesn't work all the time, so it is another useful weapon in the arsenal when it can be put to use.

One note of advice, however, to get the hang of day trading, you will have to learn more. This is attributed to the demands for pace and rapid decision-making, as well as the requirement for strong analytical skills. Often you could hear folks claim they're dealing from the gut, or they just felt like they had to get out of storage. Take them with a grain of salt, and dig into it further. Possibly these guys have had plenty of experience coping with the market or the specific product, which is why they are willing to operate on their whims and fancies, obviously. In reality, their brains have absorbed the knowledge they need, and then they can make the choices very easily.

Shorting

This side of the market carries a certain fascination and allure to certain folks, since about 50 percent of consumers are now mostly acquainted with the fact that stocks can only be acquired. They don't understand the idea that, according to trading terms and conditions, you can potentially sell short stocks that you don't buy.

Usually, short selling will enable you to sell quickly from a selection of stocks made accessible by the brokerage. This is because these are stocks that are held by the company or have received authorization from stock owners to accept borrowing. Short sellers will also be allowed to sell their non-owned securities, but would have to pay interest for the day their short positions remain operating. This same paying attention goes as we are even concerned for conditional contracts. (MFF)

Shorting as a tactic is once again part of the game that you may apply to your arsenal. Imagine the stock market situation where the bear market is just beginning. You realize that the price is going to drop by 20 percent or more, and if you have the opportunity to shorten those picked products, why not make a profit on the way down until you make the reversal and start buying the products on the cheap one?

Is it always important that you have to learn shortcut? I'd agree it's nice to know, and it's a safe choice to have available, but to be competitive in capital markets, it's not a must-have.

Taking the situation on the bear market that we spoke about earlier. If you didn't have the opportunity or simply didn't like shorting, you'd simply keep out of the market before the bear market sales kicked in and you began your long positions in your preference stocks. In the meantime, what will you do as the economy went down, you ask? You might be quietly sitting on cash doing nothing, or you could be trading in other sectors. Not all stocks work in unison, and as one is in the early stages of a bearish period, another may flow into the start of a bull run.

One thing I feel obliged to claim will be that short-term benefit appears to be higher. Exactly what do I mean?

If you were a stock too low at a certain point and you had the right call, the downward trend would typically be even smoother than if you were on the same call with the very same stock for a long time. This is why shorting income typically comes far sooner than longing income.

This stems from two primary impulses, covetousness and anxiety. In the case of shorting, the prevailing emotion that can be found on the stock exchange is anxiety. When a stock takes a dive, most committed people will not be willing to bear the impact and will want to get out fast. Their ultimate philosophy will not be to waste their capital in the stock anymore.

When we get a product that goes up in price, speculation is the biggest reason people come and drive the profit up in order that they will offer it at a better profit later on. Greed has a driving power marginally lower than terror because the human mind still needs to preserve what it has first. It cannot withstand everything it holds from separation. Therefore the fear of losing still trumps the reward greed.

That's just something you ought to take care of, but it's not a clarion call for you to leap on the shorting bandwagon anyway. I repeat that it is nice to recognize, but it is by no way sufficient for the financial markets to perform well.

Penny Stocks

When this technique really came into dominant action, I'm not aware, but to be frank, I never really used it actively. It doesn't mean I didn't take penny stock positions, but it does mean I didn't launch those positions only because they were penny stocks.

This approach relies primarily on small stocks, which are comparatively inexpensive in contrast with the more mainline stocks in play. When you take a stake in a penny stock, you will get thousands or even tens of thousands of them. The entire theory will be to wait in the market action for a tick up and then by dint of value, you are simply selling out the penny stock shares to cash in some gains.

A change of the penny stock approach will be to reach a few markets that you perceive to be positive and then buy positions of penny stocks that belong to certain businesses. This time around, the investment of penny stock wouldn't be huge, so you'd be looking for a bigger price change to understand the opportunity for benefit.

My positions in penny stocks mostly came into existence after I evaluated the stock, and I certainly didn't have the requirements that the stock could be a penny stock first.

For a cause, penny stocks adhere to the group and may vary from something like the poorly managed business to bigger structural stuff such as being in a sunset market. Performance and worth are also not to be used as the market plunge to what is called the bottom of the penny. For instance, the sector may be terribly incorrect on times, or the penny stock business is doing a great rebound.

Much of my penny deals are around the fact that businesses are always known to have any appeal and development prospects, and it is only because of seasonal causes that hammered down the market price that it counts as a penny commodity. But if I say temporary, it could be either a quick or a long wait. We never do.

As such, in my view, the penny stock investing approach isn't really one that can hold up if the scheme was solely focused on getting the stock requirements to be penny stocks.

For me, that looks so much of a risk and smacks too much expectation. Hoping that every day the stock would go up, or hoping that the market would only fall so that the whole portfolio could be sold for a benefit. If you are in stock market optimism and there is little more to support your continued interest, it should be about time to put the exit order.

Know Yourself

I realize it has been stated before, but in the light of these widely heard investing methods, I would like to hear it once again.

Many of the tactics have their applications, as we have shown. What is more relevant now is to have a clear idea of how the personality for trading is, and then pick certain tactics that you think will be a good match for you.

An individual who dislikes needing to glance at the monitors and continually being bound to the computer will be a bad match for day-trading. An individual who likes relentless action and lives for instant gratification will be a bad match for strategy in the bear market.

There are no perfect size suits all tactics out there, as it is. What would be more realistic would be to gain awareness of the various methods that you find acceptable for yourself and then turn it into a cohesive framework that can be conveniently utilized by you.

Having said that, I would like to define those traditional techniques described above as being what I might consider the tip of the iceberg. We're going to explore the investment analytics schools a bit more in detail later, and it will actually open up deeper into the investment management environment.

Strategy School Of Thought

This section can cause an explosive debate. I'm all set for it because I was selling myself through all fields of learning. This is the controversy over conceptual analyses and scientific research that is ever-present.

Before I move much further, I want to illustrate the importance of research in the field of stock picking. The findings of a well-worked and thorough study are also a building pillar that will help reinforce the judgment in moments where everybody and all is telling the contrary of what you are doing. Research offers you confidence, and you have the steady strength and capacity to ride out the turbulent waters and stop market turbulence with certainty. More specifically, you build your own understanding of stock and market place. That is still priceless. And if you might be mistaken, but the mere fact that you've developed a perspective based on a comprehensive and well-worked framework allows you the freedom to fine-tune and change your business views as the path continues.

Dream of someone who doesn't have a vision of his shoes for a while. Instead, he depends on press stories, stock magazines, and traders to fill him with suggestions of what his next major move might be. Compare it to someone who's qualified to have business understanding and angle. True, he can also collect news and investment notes, and who can claim he can't draw encouragement from these resources to find a decent invitation to stock? The main distinction is that the individual getting taught would do his own screening and a thorough examination to shape his point of view. Then he should equate his interpretation to those portrayed in the material. If divergence is clear, so he will quickly let it go.

This is in comparison to the individual who has little experience. If he's letting go of the order, he'd be concerned if the stock eventually soars to the sky, feeling regretful. And he is still traumatized by each fluctuation in rates even though he is in stock, so he loses confidence.

Proponents of basic and theoretical analyses have been at loggerheads for as long as anybody can recall. -- side strongly insists that their way of thinking is better and therefore inspires people in any path to take up studies.

I may try, for myself, to suggest that my comprehensive schooling was in the context of fundamental research. That means I was qualified in business balance sheet arithmetic and cash flow statements. We also learned to look at the business and assess its valuation so that we can foresee the course of the stock price.

It was enjoyable at school since the figures stagnate equally, and you didn't have to deal with feelings or the financial markets' hustle and bustle. Hypotheses created on paper stayed unchanged and did not alter. Company factors have not been entirely factored in yet. You didn't have cases of corruption or immoral conduct that might have a detrimental effect on market values. It was pretty tidy and sterile, with all.

Folks who believe strongly in quantitative research trust in the idea that the revenue, cash flow accounts, and the balance sheet displayed in the financial results are the key component of the puzzle they will use to break business code. They also belong to the prevailing mindset where they regard stocks as strict firms, and thus their cognitive process will revolve around evaluating the market environment and the like. Industry opportunities and entry hurdles will be at the top of their priorities if there is a decision to purchase or sell a stock.

Fundamentalists perform really well for me because they work in the context of problems that are long-lasting. The empirical bent of looking at a company's economics can take you to a filtration method. You should pick out the very powerful from the obvious ones, whilst at the same time, you might sort others who are not apparently so bad as what the market tends to decide.

As fundamentalists, we should pick out the strong firms because, in the case of some unexpected situations such as corporate abuse or exploitation, the only way is to wait for the stock to comply with the company's standards.

That is also the issue.

Often it takes a couple more times until the business catches on, then you'd be willing to enjoy the profits only for making the right choice. On some occasions, it could take you years or eons. You gladly went in with the money and, in a certain amount of time, anticipated certain benefits, and yet those hopes fall flat. The world also doesn't want to know too well what you should do! At that time, the expenditure is static, and the monies are bottled away, unable to be used elsewhere for a better future return.

In a future where there was somebody with infinite wealth, I think he'd be a really content fundamentalist because he'd be willing to deposit funds in certain businesses he'd find worth the risk and then wait for the moment to develop. Since he has nearly infinite money, he will have no concerns about the potential cost of assets. Naturally, that is the perfect setting. We exist in the modern world, and so we would have little means to name ourselves.

At this juncture, it is here where technical observers step in to point out the obvious shortcomings in the conceptual school of thinking and then rejoice in the strictly tactical trading system's apparent advantages.

At one point in my life, technological trading represented the Holy Grail for me; I was so stuck on it because I always felt that if I just discovered the right technological framework, my life would be set, and my business career would be free.

There are still several sellers of technological systems seeking to react to certain assumptions that getting "the" technical system will reflect prosperity and passive income for all the rest of eternity.

Take it from me. In trade, there is no such thing as a holy grail. In some cases, only technological processes will perform better and recover all the gains and have the losses double in other cycles. Trading algorithms can see returns in certain frames, but in others, they do offer nothing but losses.

This is not meant to break the ego, just to say the facts and what it is. For all those people who clearly claim they trust in the strength of their shifting averages, candlestick trends, and retracements of

Fibonacci, you should be fairly confident that there may be more than you can see.

I felt like an energizer bunny when I first began practicing Strategic Trading. The name of the game during those days was Back training. I'd concocted a combination of technical signals and then compare those signals back with a bunch of stocks to see the risk of loss of gain. I did it once non-stop for thirty days, and you know what, the outcome I received was a flat loss rate for a victory. That, of course, did not dissuade me in the least, since I strongly assumed that the issue resides in the concoction of technological signals, not elsewhere. As soon as I managed to create the right balance of technological signals, everything will be fine. So I thought.

It was a few years of humbling and exhausting, and at the end of my rope, as I was almost on the brink of giving up, I chanced across the idea of market action or product volume action analysis as some may term it.

The idea is that all that is to be learned regarding the stock or investment tool has already been recorded in both the price and its movement. In the case of inventories, we even have the secondary regular inventory metric is helpful proof.

This was like a letter given by a deity to one who was approaching the end of his path. It made any sense to me, at last. I didn't have to think too much about stochastics, shifting averages, and Bollinger pairs. (If all these sound like a foreign language to you, just know it doesn't matter) Price and volume will be everything I cared for.

The theory was straightforward and enticing, but in the beginning, it was very difficult when attempting to adapt to the modern world. Regulation on rates was besotted of market increases. Such market ranges were considered to be bands of assistance and opposition, and you were supposed to devise strategies to compensate for occasions when rates plummeted across certain bands or when rates rebounded away from those bands.

I've been tottering down this road for about three years, and frankly, at that point in time, it didn't appear to me I was going anywhere. If you shot a stumbling sailor in a bar struggling to rush away and catch the shuttle, it will be a detailed description of my trading experience on the equity market at the moment. It wasn't until I learned, truly learned, and held copious notes of my trade newspapers that I actually made any headway for decent benefit.

My own interpretation and usage of the basic and scientific schools of thinking will ultimately be central to targeting and filtration. I focus on the simple side of things to open up my reach and narrow down can stock I should be involved in. The technical analysis will play its role in deciding where and when the lever to join could be pulled, as well as exiting stock positions. This was a collaboration between the two great homes, and it was a lucrative arrangement that catered my tastes.

I can understand if you feel rather deflated at this stage, or maybe a little interested. Deflated because I have confirmed without a question that there is no holy grail and intrigued about what I have achieved to build the revolution for myself.

I want to repeat the section of not getting a holy grail. I say it's just not my concern if you chose not to accept that and go on splurging thousands of dollars of your hard-earned cash on folk services that try to sell you. I would just point out that if such devices perform too well, the people who market them probably won't allow you to have your hands on them. That is because the technological structures are struggling from what we term the impact of widespread use. If a certain critical mass of citizens decides to operate on the same technological signs, the exchange is essentially annulled. Even though these devices have not suffered from the consequences of widespread use, why would these people choose to sell them to you for fewer than ten thousand people a day, because they would actually create so much of a day out of these devices?

There's just no free lunch in the world at the end of the day, and if anything seems almost too nice to be true, then it generally is.

Now for the section about my success, short of sending you a personal one on a single coaching session to lead you on what works for me from a professional point of view, it's going to be really challenging to write it down because it works for you too. There are some tips I kept during the climb up, though.

Analysis of the trade journal and create links with market transactions

Reaching at the initial stage of the wider time span. You'd want to venture through the lower time frames just once you have a defined collection of guidelines and structures.

You don't need to rush; there's nothing in the universe who can push you to sell, so just take your time and start the exchange on your terms.

Please make sure to include a list of rules to obey. Even if it's only a one-liner at the outset, create the practice of making guidelines so you'll have limits within which to work.

Some Other Useful Things

I'm going to speak about certain topics in this segment that I think will be very useful to someone who wants to make more money out of trading in the stock market.

Momentum Trading

Trading and trading policy of this type depend strongly on, as the name implies, momentum. In other terms, how we build and conduct this plan will be equally contingent on purchasing or selling interest at present and planned.

Strategies may be as easy as I can commit to joining the stock the next day at the starting price if the stock has had a distance up day. This is attributed to the assumption that the trader hopes to maintain the upward trend, and therefore making such a pass. Related situations may be rendered where there has been a break in the stock down day.

Here the crux of the matter is to recognize the energy that will hopefully continue for at least a few days. A longer time will, of course, be most welcome. Sometimes, people who are only doing momentum-based trading might not have such decent win-loss percentages with their transactions, but will cover up for that with their bigger profit margins. We should not depend entirely on momentum, but rather aim to integrate it into our trading processes.

I use a motivation for the additional boost to pull in the extra money for myself. But in cases when I might have missed my goal benefit for a specific product, if I see traction in the market counter, I can only let the place continue to run.

Recognizing that certain sources of energy waves originate from the press will be the way to distinguish permanent traction from others that may fizzle out easily. Therefore it is our duty to easily and cleverly discern which bits of news have a real effect on the bottom line, and others are all everyday hogwash. Continuing to get the news that has a significant effect on the profit prospects and profitability of the business is very unusual, but we are still looking at and piece of news immediately in relation to our specific stock information. This also assumes the more acquainted you are with stock and business, the easier you'd be separating out actual news from the noise of the economy.

Trend Following

This can be considered a tactic and, at the same time, a common concept that the bulk of traders choose to obey. Trade the trend, pursue the trend, the trend is that your buddy will list among the many terms that make life better for yourself as you exchange and spend in the course of the pattern.

Only imagine it. If you have a product that has a price chart that essentially moves non-linear upward for a very long period of time, it would be fair to say that if your goal was to lengthen the product, you would have a greater chance of winning a deal.

I've been in those circumstances before, and I'll tell you it's essentially quick to only put your orders at the correct technical stage, wait for the stock price to fall back and go up to certain technical prices, and then watch your orders get filled out. After the retracement, when the market continues its upward rise, you stand by to gain a benefit or to control your portfolio positions. Benefit taking may also be an agonizing choice since you tend to lock in gains but at the same time not having to leave so much capital on the table as the stock starts to meteor upwards. Often I do it with a part of the assets gaining benefit and moving my emotional stop losses to break even with my other current section. This basically generates a concept for me that I can see the actual stock portfolios as "free" for the already earned gains charged for purchasing these new stocks. Getting free stocks doesn't imply you should handle them differently, only then there's that little extra room you're allowing yourself to gain a little less or to generate a lot of money. In certain situations, it would typically turn out to be breakeven for this free part, or I am collecting almost twice as much income as if I were trying to cut off all as a whole. My decision to undertake this step relies solely on my stock and business evaluation, as well as the existing technological condition. I would have to confess, of course, that the niggling sensation of taking a chance would typically be the main instigator for me to suggest making this leap, but the determination about whether to do so would always be focused on facts and statistics.

Trading and trading in the movement certainly has its advantages, which is why so many people expound it and even make it their slogan. But it is often challenging to understand and refine into a functioning investment plan.

One of the biggest factors being that you have to be conscious of what span of time you are on as you look at the graph.

There are numerous timescales, varying from minute charts to monthly maps. None would disagree with you that the longer the duration, the weightier such price charts will get. This is since an indicator on the month map is a reflection of the market movement for the individual stock over the entire month. The battle of the month between the bulls and the bears, as well as the cumulative total of the money they contributed to the war, are all encapsulated in that month's table. On the other side, a candle on the one-minute map will certainly have far less money invested into it relative to the month list, thereby reducing its confidence amount. Similarly, a pattern on a minute chart might be upward, but you may easily disregard the minute chart while the day chart or month chart is telling a downward tale.

Looking at higher cycle maps, such as day, week, and month levels, are best as you're starting off first. Compared to the longer time spans, the patterns depicted on these maps will have a smaller chance of turning out not to be permanent.

Another issue about pattern investing will be to have reasonable entry and exit locations. Let's say that you've finished your research and found the stock you'd like to pull the lever to enter in its upward trajectory. Currently, it is at $50 per share price. Any people could just pull the trigger and hop in at $50. Others should do what I normally do and park orders at fixed price levels that make us say $30. If the market retraces, which the market normally does, and there are barely any instances of the straight line shooting up or down, so, at a reasonable price, I'll get into stock. This also means I have nothing to risk than a person who goes in at $50 only because my price is, so to say, lower to the "park." In general, when the stock entry price is higher to the bottom, where the bottom implies $0, then you have a more secure location, just like a lower center of gravity in physics rules.

An individual purchasing at $50 or an individual purchasing at $30 will seem different only because of the various entrance rates. The $30 guy will have more leeway to transfer the product.

Think about it, if the stock price changes to $40, that's a $10 benefit for the $30 guy but a $10 loss for the $50 consumer. Naturally, a decent dose of strategic research will have to base this company with a sensible entry and exit stage. It is important to chart and decide the entrance and exit points from the technological level, and therefore the next thing to do is to have the mindset of being willing to leave the exchange.

What? What? Had I understood it, right?

Actually, you have finished. Have the emotional preparedness to leave the company. Why do you think so? This is for the occasions where the retracement exists, but it does not reach the stage, which is logically calculated. But instead of falling to $30, it rises to $33, then stages a recovery afterward. This is also valid during occasions where there is no retraction, and the market tends to rumble from $50 onwards.

You do have cases like that. Therefore, you must still be prepared emotionally to let go of the exchange and step on to the next. That is also why the investing and trading framework should never be too limiting to provide either one or two triggers every year. Imagine if you skipped the last trading chance, you might have to wait until next year to have another one.

I would also like to point out that the $50 guy might not actually be incorrect in our case, but it's just my nature to err on the cautionary side. I will tell kudos to him if the $50 guy had the gumption and the money required to handle the possible bumpier trip than the $30 guy might. What I term a "jumper" will be the $50 man. Typically these guys leap into a market out of fear of losing out. Jumpers rule the roost in moments where the movement is roaring, and the press is on the spot, which also has significant structural effects. There's absolutely no place for people who want retracements entry because there's just zero.

You either hop in that kind of circumstance, or you pass on to the next possible stock. Mentality and temperament play a major part in whether you'd be an effective jumper. And we also recognize that the nature of investing is primarily influenced by the volume of cash at stake for any particular moment in time. If you want to train yourself as a jumper and yet find yourself missing the requisite mental criteria, beginning small will be the solution. When leaping, fear tiny quantities before you get used to the sensation of it. You will also be forced to scale up to a reasonable level progressively.

I'm not much of a jumper myself, but I leap when the chance occurs. Jumping is like every other talent in the field of trade and finance, always useful to add to your arsenal so you can rely on it anytime you find you need it.

How can you decide the pattern will be another problem for some people, where others would adhere to the concept of utilizing moving averages to evaluate the pattern, and some might find Bollinger band use to be the only valid way to determine the trend?

After potentially thousands of hours staring at the maps, I've come to know that when the pattern is apparent, it's so clear that you don't require any metrics or new-catched technologies to tell you to claim this is a pattern. The Map visual analysis is what you need. I would prefer to stay on the higher time frame for me and then do a visual analysis to assess what seems like the imminent theme that is actually affecting the sector. Going from top left to bottom right will mean a downward step.

Pattern. Moving from the bottom left to the top right would indicate that the bulls will have power. If you try and search, because you can't find something that's clear, that's what we say by a trendless condition or a side sector. If a market moves sideways, that typically means the fight between the bulls and the bears is going on, and the outcomes are not yet clear.

Sideways markets are perfect circumstances for day trading, by the way, so you have what you imagine is a sort of map in a pretty rectangular type.

This ensures that the top and bottom borders are equally established for you to deal with day to day. We won't dive too much into the trading part of this day right now, maybe more in a future novel.

But there's no reason to over-complicate stuff; visual examination typically fits well since it's the easiest because when items are clear, they're generally in the truest shape.

The Need For Stop Losses

This idea was discussed at multiple junctures in this book, but I felt it's worth a segment of its own, only because of its significance in the field of trade and investment.

A stop-loss or a decreased loss is simply a fixed price point that is the escape signal for everybody to get out of a poor deal. The idea of getting a quantity that will be acceptable for the individual person to sacrifice falls into play here.

Tell Adam has decided he's willing to gamble $1000 on a certain sell offer, and he's got a hundred shares now selling at a $40 price point. It will then mean it his stop-loss price point will be at $30 if the trade call is a long one, so his risky $1000 capital would be divided by his hundred shares to produce a $10 price space. His exchange will then have space for a gyrate of up to $30, and if the price point drops below that, then he would close the deal, dust himself off, and then go ahead to the next.

This point is also the section where I would like to highlight the significance of closing the candle or bar on which you are tracking time period ever. If you're a day trader, you might be gazing at the end of the hourly light. That implies if the market price still falls below $30 on every hourly closing light, you'd be conducting the closure of the exchange. If you were a swing or long-term trader, though, you might look at the closing of the day candle or even the closing of the week candle. It would suggest you'd just conduct the exit plan when the market moves and ends on the day or week candle around $30 based on the time period you're monitoring. Keep in mind that regardless of the vast volume of money required to create and fight for the results of that specific candle, the longer the time span, the more confidence it would hold.

This argument would also contribute to another controversial field that has long been subject to discussion. Few people would say that if you chose to adopt this method, the cumulative number of damages that would be sustained would be more than the safe sum that one would spend. This is because as we are waiting for the day or week candle to end, after crashing through the predetermined point, the price may fell even further. Considering the scenario above, you could see rates at $25 or even $20 while your price range was expected to be $30. It will end in a double loss of the money you were able to fork out.

For me, I understand the drawbacks of using the stop loss in this manner, but I prefer to only do things this way because of the benefits things confers. The one big benefit you get by performing the stop loss upon closure will be that you'd be avoided circumstances when the price jumps dramatically up or down, and sometimes it doesn't close at all.

Take Adam and his stock as our example once again. The approved price for stop loss was $30. If his stock swings significantly within the hour, say $20, and yet he still tries to keep his composure and convince himself to wait until the closing hour, he may notice that at the closing hour, the stock price maybe has rebounded back to $35. And also produces what we term a pin bar or a hammer or what people might deem the candle handle.

What Adam has done by keeping his composure to get out of a condition that might have flushed his lack of stoppage. He's still in the game amid the intra-hour downward shift that turned out to be nothing but a terror.

These conditions may appear in all time frames, but keep in mind that the wider the time span, the more money to devote.

So what to do with the question of getting to pay about exactly what you were able to sacrifice initially? The solution is to transact in limited quantities. Imagine this period for Adam, instead of a hundred shares, he's only exposed to fifty shares because he knows the vulnerability of closing utilizing the stop loss, he's easily circumvented the problem, yet he's still held his safe losing number.

So when I say this, I generally get confronted with some hoots and derision, as some people would then suggest, won't the benefit opportunity be diminished similarly? The response is a yes, of course, and now I would like to inform everybody that it is all first about what you can and are able to sacrifice before we move on worrying about benefits and benefits. If we can maintain a solid basis on our expenses, so of course, gains can result. This is because the temperament for trading would be more secure and less subject to the market wind's whims and sways.

Not all, of course, subscribes to this philosophy. Others swear by the touch and go stop losing, where it simply implies that if the price ever reaches $30, as in our previous case, then the trade will end. For any span of time, there is no discussion of waiting for a close.

Under this scenario, the trader will have better control of his loss number, so his trade would be out every time $30 is reached. That also implies, however, that his odds of getting flushed out of his stop would still be much better than a trader who used the strategy of closing-stop failure.

For me, the way things are handled is not right or wrong. Often it comes down to character and psychology in dealing. I see the folks who love lots of activity are more likely to use the touch-stop method of managing stop losses, while the folks who are a bit more reserved and smoother prefer to wait for further clarification and use the close-stop loss approach as a result.

I used to subscribe to the contact pause since it was the most common and showed the most. But I didn't like the idea that I was still on the right side of the exchange only to lose it when I was pushed out of place. It's almost like a double smack on the cheek. You make a mistake because, in the trading call, you wind up being correct. That's when the near stop for me came into action, and it performed great in my view so far.

These two methods of managing stop losses are, of course, much preferable to another form of dealing stop-loss, which has no stop losses. Honestly, I can't tell it, but here's my reiteration again, there's still a stop loss, even if it's only a mental price amount. Bear the degree in mind, and you'll need to conduct the escape until it's broken. It is a fight, a war in which any exchange. If a stop-loss is broken, you realize the fight has been lost, but the fighting is always going on as long as you have the capital. Still fail to a halt.

This will be one more thing to remember. Determining the price range for a stop loss needs to make sense from the viewpoint of business research. By what do I mean? In the case of Adam, the $30 price point was calculated simply by the sum Adam was able to sacrifice and by the value of his part. This is not the way it can be, and the scenario was just kept up to demonstrate how the stop-loss could perform.

You should really keep two points in mind with a trade call first. The purchase price, or the amount you are able to pay to share in the stock's prosperity, as well as the stop loss amount calculated by the techniques of market research. In certain situations, citizens turn to scientific analyses to get a stop-loss price. They can extract price ranges from their lines of assistance and opposition and have ears identified as possible stop losses. That is also why I also point out that the task of technical analysis is more of a precision method, whereas that of fundamental analysis will be more of a filtration device to get your fine, worthwhile stocks.

This also ensures you shouldn't have too close a stop while selecting your stop-loss rate. For e.g., in the case of Adam, if his entry price was $40, and there appeared to be a slight amount of help at $38, and Adam was currently preparing his trade for the longer haul, it would be very hard to position his stop at $38. As a rule of thumb, a longer trading time will normally entail a greater loss of the pause. Similarly, if you play longer and miss a bigger rest, the benefits goals would typically be higher too. This is for each exchange to ensure a fair risk-reward ratio.

One thing I've been guilty of in the past was selecting and selecting tighter stop losses, so that helped me to have greater share visibility and thereby gain more money, at least in my opinion! I'd pick a close stop and then genuinely hope the economy doesn't hit that amount. Any of my trades have been so unbelievably organized that I will be in a deal and then out of business within a few minutes, with a few hundred losses to match. This was especially so whilst I was still doing the lack of contact pause. It doesn't make sense to look fine on paper and assume the economy doesn't affect the lack of the end. Also, beginning to calculate the gain right before beginning the exchange is no good. Engaging in mental gymnastics like that will just waste your focus and leave you empty when you need it.

That is why virtually all trades that end up as winners start with the first issue of how much we might lose. All that's on offer is truth and statistics and less optimism and wishful thinking. It's crucial that we perceive things as what they are and not what we expect them to be.

Stock Screeners

These items are so popular these days, with most of them being accessible through web browsers and online. The primary usage of stock screeners will be to have some sort of automatic support while we deal with the boring task of searching out filtering firms.

With only a few mouse clicks, screeners will support a lot in this world with hundreds of thousands of stocks, and we'll have a more accessible shortlist of a handful of hundreds. Okay, it was almost a half-joke, but to be frank, occasionally, you still had to dig around a couple of hundred businesses to get to some deserving of being sold.

Insiders and Institutional Investors

As well as being the hard weights, these guys are also the ones who know most about their businesses. Knowing their records will give us a big leg up for institutional investors when it comes to our investment decisions.

Looking at individual pages documenting those trends and also reading the annual reports to get a sense of who is who and who is doing what would be nice, but it could create too much of a cognitive challenge. Imagine tracking the shortlist of fifty individual securities and maintaining track of insider and retail activity. That pushed the wall toward me.

An easier approach I find for myself would be to use the professional analysts' concept and trust it. The stock price has all caught that which needs to be understood. I keep on board the notion when it comes to tracking products that have already been shortlisted. Yet when it comes to getting the shortlist together, there's simply no moving away from the hard legwork that comes with the foundational research.

For me, fundamental analysis with its regular hard work would guide the way in the development of my monitoring shortlist of stocks; then, technical analysis would offer me the degree of pricing to implement my investing ideas.

Chapter 13: Common Mistakes to Avoid and Suggestions

If stocks move up, down, and sideways it is possible to benefit by selling options. With a fairly tiny cash outlay, you might use option methods to sell stocks, preserve gains and control huge parts of the stock.

Sounds nice, doesn't it? Here we have the pick.

You may also risk more by buying options than the overall sum you've spent over a fairly short span of time. That is why continuing with caution is so necessary. Also, self-confident investors will misjudge a chance and lose capital.

It addresses the top 10 errors that novice options traders usually make, with professional advice from our in-house advisor, Brian Gitomer, about how you might trade wiser. Take time now to study them, so you can prevent an expensive wrong move.

Misaligned Leverage

Many rookies abuse contracts providing leveraging factor alternatives without knowing how much chance they are taking. They're also attracted to making quick-term calls. So, this is so often the case; it's important to ask: Is it a "speculative" or "conservative" strategy to buy outright calls?

Leverage of a Master. A general rule to start option investors: if you're usually trading 100 stock lots, then stay with one start option. When you usually exchange 300 lots of securities-maybe three agreements. That is a decent volume of training to start with. When you don't have luck on small scales, the bigger scale trades would more definitely not be successful.

Not Being Responsive to New Initiatives

Most option traders claim they'd never purchase out: of-the-money stocks or offer the options in-the-money. Such absolutes sound stupid – till after you find oneself in a market that is working against you.

There have also been experienced options for investors. Confronted by this situation, you are sometimes inclined to violate all kinds of ethical rules.

You have also learned, as a bond investor, a common excuse for scaling up to keep up. For e.g., if you loved the stock when you purchased it at 80, at 50, you have to love it. It may be enticing to purchase more on the exchange to reduce the total cost level. However, be vigilant: In the field of options, what provides a sense for shares does not float. Typically, boosting up as a potential tactic just doesn't make any sense.

Be accessible to exploring different approaches to invest in futures. Note, options are securities, implying that their values don't shift the same or have almost the same characteristics as the stock market. A decline in time, whether positive or poor, for the role, must also be taken into account in the strategies.

When things will change in your business, and you contemplate what was previously inconceivable, just honestly ask yourself: was this a move I took when I first started opening this status?

If the reaction is no, so do not.

Close a trade, cut down on your damages, or start a different chance that makes perfect sense today. Options give decent leverage opportunities on comparatively low assets, but when you dig deeper, they can explode just as rapidly as every position. Take a minor risk because it presents you with an opportunity to eventually escape a disaster.

Wait Much long to Order Limited Options

This failure can be distilled down with one word of wisdom: Always be eager and able to buy out shorter options soon.

Too many traders may take too long to purchase back their sold options. There are many million explanations for doing this. For instance:

- You don't want the tribunal to the bill.
- You're hoping that the deal ends void.
- You're only looking to get a bit more from the exchange.

Just when to give the short options back. If OTM gets lost with your short alternative and you can purchase it back to profitably, take the danger off the table, do it. Don't be greedy about that.

For example, what if you offered a choice for $1.00, and now it's worth 20 percent? To start with, you wouldn't offer a 20: cent option, as it would just not be worth it. Equally, you must not believe scraping out the remaining few cents from this deal is worth it.

Here's a simple thumb rule: if you may keep 80 percent or more of the original income from the choice deal, you can definitely buy it back. This is a virtual guarantee, otherwise. A few of these weeks, you'll bite back by a short choice because you took too long.

Putting in Spreads

Many traders with starting options seek to "pull-in" a gap by first purchasing the choice and then selling a second choice. They seek to cut the amount by a handful of pennies. That's just not worth the chance.

Comfortable sound? That example has also fried most seasoned options traders and taught the valuable lesson.

When you decide to swap a set, don't "jump in" Deal one set as a one-time deal. Don't needlessly take on excessive business pressure.

You could purchase a call, for instance, and then seek to schedule the selling of some other call, trying to get out of the second leg a little bit better. If the economy experiences a fall, this is a risky tactic, because they won't be capable of carrying off the profit. You may be faced with a call option with little plan to move on.

If you're trying the whole strategic plan, don't buy the spread but also wait approximately, hoping the economy will be moving in the favor. You may imagine you might market it at a better price later. This is a rather unlikely performance.

Also, view a split as one deal. Don't want to solve the pacing minutia. Before the economy keeps going down, you should get into a trade.

Ignoring the Stocks for Fair Markets Table

Person inventories may be very unpredictable. For instance, if a company has a large unpredicted news event, this could rock a stock for a couple of days. On the other side, even extreme chaos in a large company that is a member of an

S&P 500 will certainly not trigger the index would fluctuate significantly.

What Are the Story's Morals?

Options trading focused on benchmarks will protect your part from the tremendous changes that individual news reports may produce for selected securities. Take into account neutral transactions on big indicators, and reduce the unsure impact of news from the market.

Find investment tactics that may be lucrative if the sector already sits on indices, including a short break (also named margin requirements). Index moves appear to be much less intense than some other methods and far less likely to be impacted by media.

Traditionally, the short spread is built for income, even though the fundamental value stays the same. Short position spreads are thus deemed "fair to bearish," and short puts spread are "good to bullish." This is one of the main distinctions between longer spreads or short spread.

Note, spreads include trading in greater than one alternative and thus incur and over one fee. Hold that in factors when choosing the choices on trade.

Not Realizing What to Do at the Task

If you offer options, just periodically inform yourself that you may be allocated early, until the expiry date. Most new retail investors never dream about assigning as a prospect before such time that it occurs. When you haven't factored into the assignment, it can be confusing, particularly if you are operating a multi-leg approach like short or long spreads.

For instance, what if you run a call option spread and are given the short higher-strike option? Starting traders may panic or exercise the long option to utilize the stock for the lower hit. This is definitely not the right choice, though. Selling the long choice on the stock market, taking the residual time premium together with the intrinsic interest of the contract, and utilizing the profits to purchase the order, is typically cheaper. Then, at a higher price, you will buy the company to the individual investor.

An early appointment is one of the often-unpredictable market activities which are genuinely emotional. When it occurs, there is always no rhyme or explanation behind it. It is all true. And as the economy shows, it's a trick less than genius.

If delegated well in advance, go about what you will do. The greatest defense towards the early task is to let it play into your early thought. Otherwise, it will lead you to make less than rational, in-the-moment, protective decisions.

Taking consumer dynamics into account will aid. -- one is more prudent to work out early, for example? A call or a put? Trying to exercise a put or stock sale right ensures the dealer sells the stock or gets cash.

Always question yourself: Do you like your money now or when it expires? Citizens often prefer cash now or cash later on. This implies the puts appear to be more prone to earlier activity than calls.

A calling implies that the dealer must be able to invest cash to buy the product relative to the game later. Waiting for and investing the cash later is typically human nature. When an inventory is rising, though, less qualified traders can squeeze the pin early, lacking to know that they are leaving a certain time premium mostly on the table. How will an early task be random?

Failure of Reality for Next Event

Not all market developments are predetermined. However, there are two important things to keep on top of while selling options- profits and dates of dividends on the stock market.

For starters, if you've sold puts and a payout is coming, it improves the chances that you may be allocated early because the choice is already in cash. This is particularly true if we consider the dividend to be increasing. That's the proprietors of options that have no dividend protection. Options traders will exercise the right to receive, and by the common assets.

Make sure things weigh pending. You'll need to learn the former-dividend date, for starters. Stay well clear of offering put options with unpaid distributions, unless you are able to consider higher assignment costs.

Trading with the company's securities during the price action normally ensures that you may face greater uncertainty - and therefore pay an elevated cost for that opportunity. If you intend to buy a choice during the profit-taking, then one choice is to buy another option and offer another, producing a spread.

Illiquid Options Trading

Cash flow is about how fast a trader could even buy this without causing major movement in price. A smart investor is one that often contains available, committed sellers and buyers.

Here's a way to talk about everything: Liquidity relates to the possibility the next transaction can be carried over at a rate equivalent to the previous.

Options markets are, for one basic explanation, more competitive to option markets. Investment bankers swap only one stock, while rational investors can select from hundreds of strike prices.

For instance, investment bankers would rush to one type of, let's just assume, IBM stock; however, brokerage firms may have six separate expirations to choose from a host of strike rates. By nature, further choices imply that the price action would generally not be as competitive as the equity market.

A good reason like IBM is not normally a liquidity issue for stock traders and options traders. Narrower inventories creep into the issue. Take extreme Green Technologies, an environmentally sustainable (imaginary) energy business of some hope, can have only one stock that sells once per week by request.

The stocks on extreme Green Technologies are likely to be much more negative if the portfolio was illiquid. Typically, this will allow the gap between the offer and leading to a "to have the options excessively high.

For e.g., whether the bid-ask difference is $0.20, then if you purchase the contract $2.00, that's a maximum of 10 percent of a price charged to determine the place.

It's never a smart decision to place your role right away at a 10 percent loss, even by picking a highly leveraged alternative with a broad bid-ask range.

Trading overleveraged options push up the expense of doing so, and on a yearly basis, price action prices are now greater than stocks. Don't place yourselves on a load.

If selling stocks, please ensure that the available position is at least 40 times the size of the connections that you choose to sell.

For e.g., to exchange a 10-lot, the appropriate leverage must be 10 x 40, or perhaps a minimum of 400 open interest. Open value reflects the number of option contracts left with a market price and expiry date that were bought or exchanged to put it up. Any closing payments raise the open value, although it reduces the closure of payments. Also, at the end of each financial day is measured the free interest. Invest liquidity options to avoid extra expenses and pressures on yourself. There are tons of possibilities somewhere for liquids.

Search for resources that can assist you in discovering possibilities, obtain perspective, or respond when the urge attacks? Find out our Trade platform's smart devices.

Doesn't Have an Escape Route

You have always seen it before, a thousand times. It's important to manage the emotions when bulk purchases, much like stocks. That does not involve swallowing all the worries in a human - level way. It's far better than all that: Get a job schedule and adhere to it.

You have to have an escape schedule, time frame. Except though things fall at your side. Use an upside-out stage, a downward escape stage, and well-advanced timescales for each departure.

What if you head out though early and drop it upside hand on the ground?

That is the preoccupation of a traditional dealer. Here's the perfect counterpoint: what about if you reliably made a profit, then the frequency of injuries, and sleep well at night?

Establish a strategy for the exit. Whether you purchase or sell shares, an escape strategy is an utter necessity. This lets you develop more efficient trading patterns. This, therefore, maintains some power over the fears.

Evaluate an upside-down escape strategy, but the worst-case situation you're able to accept. If you accomplish your objectives on the upside, transparent your place, and take all your money. Don't feel gloat. If you hit your stop-loss downside, you can clear your place once again. Don't subject yourself to unnecessary danger by betting that the price of the right can return.

Perhaps from start to end, the urge to break this guidance will be high. Use so not. You have to build a decision, but instead commit to it. All too many merchants draw out a schedule and then throw the strategy to suit their impulses as long as the exchange is done.

Call Options for (OTM)

Buying OTM strikes openly is some of the most challenging ways to reliably earn money in options trading. Margin requirement sell options cater to traders of fresh options since they are inexpensive.

Begin would seem like a reasonable place: Purchase the best escorts alternative and see whether you can select a winner. Calls to purchase should sound comfortable as it fits the trend you're used to pursuing as a stock trader: trade away and seek and sell big. Yet if you restrict yourself to that technique alone, you will continually lose capital.

Try offering an OTM long position on an already held portfolio as the first approach. This method is regarded as a strategic concealed call.

What's good with protected calls as a tactic is that if the call is secured by a cash position, the danger will not arise from buying the right. This even has the ability to give you market profits while you're optimistic but also able to sell the shares if the price goes up. This tactic will give you the "look" of how contract rates for the OTM option shift when the approaches to expiry and the changes in market demand.

Nonetheless, the danger resides in controlling a stock - as well as the danger may be big. Although offering the covered call does not create capital danger, it does reduce the upside, thereby increasing the possibility of opportunity. If the price increases and your request is executed, you face needing to buy the shares after the assignment.

Chapter 14: Facts and Numbers to Help You

This field is where we dive further into the fascinating environment of quantitative stock market research. It will be to look through the business figures and sort them out and see if they're making the grade for us to track. Often the main issue is how we can manage this?

The Value Question

This is probably one of the first items you'll experience when you run across someone who looks at the financial market from a fundamentalist's eyes. Does this business show worth, and is the worth that the investment market already realizes?

Some people live and breathe the notion that for trading in the stock market, you should depend entirely on fundamentals. They're not perfect. I've seen and been in contact with individuals who have never seen a stock chart in their life and who have gone on to create millions in capital market transactions. The following are among the more popular denominators among these people:

Compared to the regular street Joe, they begin with more than usual amounts of capital.

As a result, they seem to have an overall stronger grasp on their trading psychology

On days where the stocks have dramatic swings, they prefer to make their profits, which implies they are certainly not day traders or short term buyers.

Occasions that come to mind are like the collapse of the 2000 software bubble, as well as the turmoil of the 2008 mortgage notes, or the Lehman case.

They don't need to depend on the profits for their everyday life and expenditures from their savings.

Fundamentals may be all you need to move ahead in the stock market investment sector. You use basics to pick up a decent product and then steadfastly wait for either the stock price to be down so that you can purchase the stock or sell it as the general demand becomes excessively buoyant to cash in on the greed of others.

It would require lots of patience, and then you will have to wait for the unspecified incident that will push the market price below the valuation you realize it has. Typically no brainers will be global incidents, impacting the entire financial price and getting the blow from both counters. This is how it influences all counters because the anxiety is too prevalent, without even waiting for any reasoning or thinking. This also suggests that the rates being depressed are more likely to only be influenced by expectations than to have some specific systemic problems inside the business. If the incident is only based on the particular business, perhaps further brain work will be required to sift through the evidence and noise and decide if the importance you've seen of the organization before still remains.

Investing in fundamentals is just a waiting process, where you are waiting to get in, and then you are waiting to get out again. It's not cut out for all people, to be frank. I mean, if we look at a typical scenario in a regular middle-class household when both parents are going off work, and you realize they get some extra cash every month that they put into their bank account. For some people who might have built up a modest nest egg of say $50,000, it will be simple to tell on paper, but tougher to do without some sort of work, as market prices are still poor.

Perhaps these people will be best off getting regular exposure and studying as well as knowing more about their mindset in investment and selling, which would then bring them in a far healthier spot through major openings provided in periods of financial turbulence.

Think also about the individual who wants to exchange today, since he might have a large amount to start with, but because of his choice to depend on that amount to produce his monthly profits, this fundamental investment approach will not be fast enough to maintain a healthy lifestyle.

But my opinion is that basic expenditure is all fine and can function well on its own two feet. It is about carrying a blade to a fight. It is a dignified tool to use. And I am posing this issue to you now. Why carry one blade if you can handle two?

My personal understanding of this is what I stated in the other segments earlier. For filtration purposes, I use fundamental research since it is the inherent power when looking at the fundamentals. You will see the power and competencies of an organization when it comes to figures and annual accounts. This means I'm just going to limit my trading and investment shortlist to businesses with a strong and proper role. I mean, if we're interested in Starbucks, we should actually summarize their company as selling coffee, and that's how we'd mold our thought and look at their business model's other aspects.

Getting the sword of fundamental analysis with you allows you the opportunity to select and choose from the vast pool of stock candidates out there, and that will improve your winning chances. And yeah, I'm going to remove the gun comparisons right here and now, in case it could annoy any people.

For instance, the other tool I would use besides reading the basics would be to use scientific research or map reading, as others might term it. If fundamentals provided the barrier, you would store and pick your businesses with, so the strategic analysis will provide you the timing and signals to take them out of the water and communicate with them.

One gives you a filtration device; the other gives you an interaction method.

Let's look at what we normally search for in a business and decide whether it is worthy of reflecting worth.

Increasing Profits

Profits reflect growth, and growth typically brings value to people like us investing in the stock market, which translates into a winning investment. What's better than winnings? Well, yields are growing year after year. That would actually be great news for any vested individual whose firm is seeing such development.

Usually, benefit numbers under the portion of the income statement can be conveniently accessed from the company's annual reports. Most reports these days offer at least a one-year comparison with the most recent collection of figures released, but that would not be enough. For the people who deign not to use the power of the internet, they will then hopefully have to collate and click through all the company's actual annual reports for ten years. It would be much better if you could get fifteen. Note, with their deep learning algorithms, when we have more data, our brain behaves like those of artificial intelligence, we consume and can process more.

I used to enjoy doing this, and I just like flipping through papers. There was something about the paper and its scent that just attracted me to it. But I have to admit, it's been hard work. Honest. You'd probably start looking at stars after you walked through three businesses. That is why I would urge everyone to make use of the technology that we all have at our disposal. You can easily look at a firm's ten-year results these days and focus on its profit metric.

A good measure will be a situation in which you see a steady development year after year. Usually, this informs you that the business has stable profits and is still expanding to meet the demand opportunity at the same time. For the gross profit, we will keep an eye out while paying more attention to the net profit figure. We want to see what the revenue and product costs are even for the business. That way, you will work out the profitability of the business, and that can be a helpful thing to have in your mind.

I have my sensors put out when I see steady growth that is then punctuated by a sudden spurt of growth. To be honest, I just don't like those circumstances and would most certainly need to take a closer look at them. This is the time that you really first got to get through the annual reports, potentially using at least three annual reports. I still take the previous annual report, the yearly growth spurt report, and the yearly report afterward. You'd like to explore what caused the growth spurt, and if it were sustainable, the main question would be. Many businesses have such spurts on paper, and it shows up extremely well, just to make it revealed later that a one-off sale of some commodity actually made money. It is our responsibility to find out what is happening, and to make informed, accurate decisions for ourselves, as it will build up our confidence as we move to the process of decision making.

Increasing Sales

The income or sales figures may also forecast the profits, and certain businesses report their sales statistics but do not book the profits until after the distribution of the programs or products. Revenue figures will be a decent benchmark for measuring any business, and, of course, we would like to see a year-on-year rise in sales as evidence of having a growing business in our sights.

For certain businesses, there might be little to no improvement in their revenue and profit figures, maybe one or two percent a year. Counters like Macdonald's would come to mind, and General Electric would. There are more secure, steady counters who have engaged their potential in the market and are likely to just cruise along. What they signify to the investor will be cash in dividend forms, as well as value development by company stock purchase backs. If well managed, these behemoths will typically sit on cash stockpiles, which are generally distributed to shareholders as dividends or used in acquisitions of corporate stocks.

Corporate stock acquisitions tend to raise the stock price per share as sales decrease the total number of stocks on the market.

Then others would wonder, what's the point of looking at such slow-growing firms? Recall,

Our job is to identify and filter those companies that are well run and meet our target pool criteria. Although these bigger businesses do not have the revenue and profit growth rates, they do show value when they have stock price depressions due to either external or internal shocks. That's why it's also a good idea to have a grasp on what would be a reasonable price for these stocks because you'd know whether it's under- or overvalued.

Granted, if we were able to choose, it would be fantastic to go every day of the year for growth firms, particularly when we are on the path to building more financial capital. For those that have a better slice of the pie or maybe a slice of silver or gold in the spoons that have been used to feed you, then the bigger firms with larger and more stable dividend payouts might make sense to park some money there.

For me, you will see steady growth year after year when it comes to measuring the revenue and benefit figures. It can be, but not super popular. Then what do you do with figures getting their ups and downs? A simple rule of thumb is to determine how many down years in the ten-year cycle are present. If it's more than three, I won't look too much into it, unless all those three years were packed closer to the front together, and the more recent figures are all showing steady progress.

The main point that I want to impress on everyone here is that with these numbers and details, we're trying to construct a narrative. No airy-fairy castles, just good old strong facts, and figures in the dream sort of thing. A business with some dips and some development unexpectedly punctuated over a span of ten to fifteen years will send a message to me that either there is something wrong with the company's management, to it's in a cyclical industry. If, after learning all of these, we are still interested in the business, then we will have the means to further investigate.

I want to go down the least road of resistance when it comes to me, though. What this means is that I would prefer to trade or invest in a business with steady growth, as seen in their 10-year study, rather than in a business with splotchy growth estimates. Some could argue. Yes, I may miss out on the unpolished gem, and yes, sometimes these splotchy numbers of growth actually mean something better. I still think, though, that with the universe of stocks as it is, there will always be a great chance for me to rope in the gains just as well as riding on the growth firms. You could call me lazy, but just me. In searching for the no-brainer growth stocks, I prefer to dump more effort than to spend effort investigating if a splotchy one is worth the hit.

Low Liabilities

We looked at revenue and benefit figures, but now we're going to look at the company's obligations and assets we may be involved in. It is important to take care of two main items for this chapter. The liability or obligations in the long run and the present liability.

We would prefer to see the capital flow of the business is sufficient to pay down the entire outstanding obligations with the existing liability, which is generally defined by the liability where the creditors will become callable within a year. The higher the cash-to-current debt ratio is, the lower we will score the business.

We typically use this formula debt - to - equity for the long-term loans to see the future health situation for the company we are investing in. Equity is the company's equity belonging to the owners, who are people like you and me. In this situation, we like the amount to be as little as practicable, so it will mean that the liability owed to creditors is even smaller than the worth we shareholders assign.

It's also a positive situation to have less leverage in the business since it means that the company does not need to draw into leverage yet to boost its expansion. This usually occurs when the business is in a fast-growing market with lots of demand or where the business has high barriers to entry into the goods or services and is willing to dictate competitive rates.

But ultimately, both firms seem to hit a point where they will find it easier to take on debt to finance their growth plans. The key here is that we don't want a possible goal organization to get pulled into a leverage pit where they take on too much leverage for their own gain. A debt-to-equity level of about 0.5 or less will be a fair gauge of what we strive to accomplish.

We really don't want to see a scenario in which the business simply requires loans to cover its operational expenses. This is typically a negative indication since it simply shows that regular net revenues or cashflow alone cannot cover the operational costs. This does not mean, though, that the business is beyond repair, as I saw companies who managed to achieve turnarounds after being saddled with debts. Speaking of shorting or short selling these businesses is indeed foolhardy, as I have seen too many people talking. If I can't purchase those businesses, why shouldn't I sell them short instead? Not many of these debt-saddled companies run the risk of falling under their own weight. For years or even decades, they will even be able to maintain this illusion of reputable activity, but it will be foolhardy to shorten these businesses only on the grounds of just one debt measure.

Increasing Return On Equity

The return on equity is the firm's operating earnings essentially measured by the owners' cumulative capital credited. This number reflects how much the capital will have played in the shareholder pot in the previous year. Higher net earnings would mean a greater yield, which would also imply a happier opportunity for the owners. I say, more value for one buck, right?

That this statistic is important is also attributed to the company's probability of offering stock. As stock redemption arises, the cumulative amount of trading securities is raised, which therefore means that the firm's gross asset valuation will rise as well. If the income of the business were to rise at a constant pace, yet would be faced with only a raise in equity that would be very bad news that more hands must share the gains.

A growing return on equity ratio will therefore be a very welcoming sight since it basically implies that the business is allowing greater use of its investments to produce further gains for its stockholders.

Perhaps, some people may wonder, does this same problem of making more people exchanging earnings arise during a market split? The direct response is no, and this is why. A stock split is effectively a scenario when a $100 per share is divided into usually two pieces, producing a scenario where after the break, it becomes $50 apiece. No extra capital appreciation is injected to expand the investor base.

Barriers to Entry

Another consideration to weigh for determining a stock's profitability will be the qualitative element of the entry barriers. How difficult will it be for rivals to join the same room with that business to offer a free for all?

Take Starbucks, for example, what it's offering goes beyond a cup of high-quality coffee. It's really offering the atmosphere of Starbucks that occurs anytime all of its consumers walk into the shop. I say coffee is simple to make, correct? You might do that on your own, but why would you actually want to skip down to a Starbucks store to have them produce the particular coffee and then charge you a premium for it? That in itself is one of Starbucks' effective entrance barriers as good protection against it will be competitors.

Barriers to entry cannot often be caused by the business. They could very well be

Government policy outcomes. For this case, let's go a bit afield here. They have a federal law in the South East Asian nation of Singapore, which requires all vehicles that are three years of age or older to go to an authorized agent for annual vehicle inspection. Only say what? In the nation, there are just a few such approved agents around, and that essentially renders it an oligopoly. To add to the appeal of this sector, it is a well-known reality that it is almost difficult to get the government to approve another new worker.

If you were an investor looking at this sort of situation, only concentrating on the entry factor barriers will send you very optimistic vibes on that. In a market with only two participants, you have a government regulation that practically guarantees demand for the services that are rendered. Some may be inclined to draw comparisons with Boeing and Airbus, but in reality, the business these two behemoths work in is very different in nature. Purchases of aircraft appear to be cyclical in nature, with airlines preferring to put their fleet orders in the estimation of how their potential demand will be. As such, aircraft manufactures are therefore exposed to this cyclical stream of demand, which is ebbing and flowing. The market there is a relative constant for the automotive inspection industry. When the next customers come, you don't have to think.

Another form of hurdle will be the high expense of change, whether the consumer wants to move from one brand to another. This is true; just think about converting your desktop to mac. I think if you're a good member of the dual method, then kudos to you. And those born and raised on the computer, converting to the mac is sort of like giving birth, rough and unpleasant. Perhaps it will feel like a change for those who have been weaned on the mac to move into the computer.

We aim to have enterprises with as low entry obstacles as possible or just a few really high obstacles to get businesses. This means that due to potential competitors, the market that the prospective target firms are in will not be overcrowded out too fast. However, one point to remember is my belief that there would be no obstacle forever to end. Stuff often comes about, shifts in political policy, disrupts the infrastructure.

Any of these variables will induce transition and generate a ripple impact that breaks down a barrier's once strong fortress.

So the key here is to move into businesses that have strong barriers in effect and then see how the management is building paths to developing new barriers in readiness for the day that their existing barriers become redundant. I will call this a positive thing to have, but not specifically important in the initial stages of stock filtration.

Why? For what?

Just because you begin to weigh too many driving forces and mechanisms, there will actually be information overload. Attempting to see what one company's management is doing may be feasible, but it would seem utterly arduous because you have to do it regularly for five to six hundred years. When it falls into effect, there will be a real danger of getting complacent. In an allotted period of time, you have so many businesses to dig at that the brain would be tempted to stop the phase shortly. In doing so, it will sacrifice the normal robustness and close evaluation as well as the study of expression.

This is why I would advise people to work on looking for the obstacles to entry first, without knowing whether any proposals for potential barriers are being drawn up by management.

Another item to consider would be a simple heading. You certainly don't want to start considering entrance hurdles simply because you're too besotted with some single business. In general terms, the simpler the definition of the entry obstacle, the easier and better it can be. Anybody should attempt to describe it. Even better if the individual has an utter zero business or stock awareness. If they can see what you're attempting to convey in the shortest practicable period, in terms of the power and simplicity of the entrance barrier, you might have a champion here.

Management

The company's executive staff will be directly linked to access obstacles in dispute. It can also be classified as one of the barriers to entry if this element is considered to be high.

Much as the captain who is navigating the ship on the seas, the organization's manager or decision-maker will be equally responsible for bringing the corporation into the choppy market waters. A good, competent captain would ensure the safety and stability of the company, as would successful management.

The main problem here is to understand how to properly define effective and powerful governance. I say, for the most part, we're individual buyers, not hedge fund traders like Peter Lynch who can jet around the world and show in for a peek at the business headquarters. The good part here is, there aren't many items in this day and age of social networking that can't be ferreted out if you're of a mind.

We Take a Look at Their Track Record

Simply key their names into Google, and you should at least be able to take a whiff if they have some managerial expertise of some sort. Taking a glance at the present status of their former businesses and often take into consideration what their exit date was and traceback performance records of four to five years prior to transferring.

Another factor is looking at their specific interests about where they are living and what they are doing. Personally, with those people who are a bit more down to earth and a little less glamorous, I am more of a fan. That's not to suggest I haven't seen home runs with glamorous, noisy people operating businesses; it's just my own choice.

Generally speaking, I prefer to think that those who are a little less vocal will usually allow their acts to come out. They don't need huge mansions and flash cars but just let their performance speak for themselves. To take the famous Warren Buffett as an illustration, we won't have to search for it. Yeah, you might say he's an intense mite because the universe really doesn't allow them that way anymore. Ok, many other people are models with the less glamorous lifestyle, and I'm sure you can recognize them.

Another thing I would like to find out is the boy with the hand of the Midas. There's still somebody like that, obviously. An individual who suddenly turns around a worn-out corporation starts up new enterprises and immediately becomes a success. I'd like to concentrate more on the figures and hard data while the organization has such a dynamic boss. The reason I'm concerned about the company's value is something factor in the star leader's "light," because if that light is no longer available, the stock might take a dive. Often, when we meet such a dynamic man, there may be all-around encouraging reviews that can cause us to get quickly swept away at the moment we feel good. I'm still suspicious of this, but I'm going to try to use statistics and evidence to anchor myself. If there are not enough figures, so I'll prefer to miss the business and follow the next better one.

Valuation

This may be a multi-billion dollar issue when it comes to simple research. Both funnies will like a figure that they can use to equate with the actual price of the trade. That's how people come up with words like under-or-above-value. The index to which the selling price is measured will be the amount deriving from the valuation.

So then, how do we extract the valuation number? If you were to conduct a quick google search, it turns out that you would be able to pull up at least three or four common forms of valuation approaches that Wall Street analysts are expected to use. Let's speak a little about them here, about the processes, not the specialists on Wall Street.

Next up will be the patriarch of both of them, the discounted study of cash flow. It's a process that requires several digits, as the name implies, and if you had to punch the digits on a calculator manually, it could take you a little while to hit your final destination. Believe me; I've done it before.

Luckily, we have outstanding spreadsheets and a plethora of other technical miracles that will simplify this phase for us to reduce the main numbers we are concerned about.

We would like to see what the company's actual net cash flow is. From the new annual accounts, that can be conveniently downloaded, so no issues here. The next number in question will be the expected pace of growth that you would like to add to the mentioned business.

How we will measure this will usually be to provide data worth about ten years in terms of sales and benefit. Then we review the growth rates periodically and take an average of nine years. If we have reasonable growth rates both in sales and benefit, the sensible course of action will be to choose the lower of the two ratios. I say, in most situations, to be careful is often safer. However, some people appear to be a little more a purist when it comes to that stuff, but they carry yet another combination of the two figures. However, as the case might be, the end goal will be to obtain a forecast pace of growth for the business that can fairly be counted upon.

I claim fairly since there's no one on earth who can guess what the company's real growth pace would be. So many variables on hand may confuse the count, and we're going to have to make do with the strongest estimates we may obtain.

After the company's growth pace, we'll also have to determine the correct discount rate, which is typically the capital expense required to finance to run the business. For that, there's a sophisticated word named WACC. Simply it implies weighted average capital expenditure. There are equity and debt both in business. The loan expense will be the interest rate paid to the business by the lending sector. Think about the mortgage, which helps you to raise funds to acquire your house or vehicle. You have to pay tax on certain accounts. The same goes for the corporation, and the cost of debt will be the average interest. Equity expenses will be just the total yield on equity. WACC is then determined by taking correct debt and equity ratios over the company's net asset valuation and calculating the related costs.

While it's not particularly relevant about what we do, the purist in me just had to bring that out for the record. And WACC as well will be determined.

Equity Valuation Divided By Net Asset Value Multiplied by Expense Of Equity + Debt Value Divided By Net Asset Value Multiplied by Debt Expense Multiplied by One Half of the prevailing tax rate.

There you have it. Only knock out with WACC.

But since we have these three significant figures in discounted cash flow analysis, it will be sort of simple to produce the absolute golden number, which is basically the final amount of all operational cash flows carried out into the future using the expected growth rate, and discounted back into the present using the WACC.

Another way to arrive at the value figure will be by calculating price-earnings or multiples. In short, the PE ratio is assumed to be the product of dividing the market price by earnings per share of the stock.

Once again, some people will use around ten years of statistics to figure out the cumulative PE amount and add it to the actual earnings per share and get an idea of what the company's future worth could be.

If you are not still floating in a lot of ifs, buts, and expectations, it would be high time to realize that when doing DCF and even PE valuation, you would be doing a lot of that. And if the financial model may be complex at the end of the day, the fundamental reality is that it will still be based upon assumptions. Hypotheses that could be changeable or volatile because of the mere reality that we tend to look so much into the future.

Let's face it, in the seventies, people would actually have had a fair idea of what lifestyle might be like in the eighties. Now people would actually have a difficult time predicting how things might work out to be like in the next ten years. Technology is both the maker and the killer with the introduction of self-driving vehicles, artificial intelligence, and deep learning. Who is to claim you can't ruin or rebuild a company's expectations and dreams?

I mean, to be talking like this right now may sound like a super wet blanket. I say, maybe you should go, but what's the point of performing all those fundie analyzes? Everything goes down the pipe, and we can't foresee the future. Don't worry.

A preliminary reference for us would also be DCF or PE, or other kinds of financial models that pump out valuation figures. It is by no way the entirety of the decision-making phase to be the finish. If we get a DCF valuation figure, we have a very vague understanding of whether this business is above or underpriced at the moment. Our key foundation is to always process and shape a pool of prospective target firms utilizing all the fundamental facets of the research listed above. Going at progress from the viewpoint of sales and benefit, taking in qualitative factors as well as rounding things off with the value figures, it will be customized to the variety of businesses. We are not going to make judgments on purchasing or selling based on valuation amounts.

Chapter 15: Constant Profits

This section would explain how to stay ahead in terms of profiting from the stock market. We still say stuff like, a number of times:

Many investors struggle to make profits off the equity market, even more so for retail companies, but at the end of the day, the house still wins

It is safer to put your trust in mutual funds and highly paid professionals

In most marketing materials for pricey stock trading and investing classes, this will be the moment where the content will say categorically that they had the unique response that would allow you to be the lucky one or ten percent who would reliably beat the market, harvest passive gains, all on a simple one-hour investing a day.

Sounds amazing, right?

The reality is that many supermarket companies are losing money, but many are still earning profits, and the only ones who would actually know for sure will be the tax department officials. As I said, the path from the stock market to gain and prosper lies primarily with yourself.

In order to study to appreciate how the competition operates, you have to invest in the time and commitment to have a fair chance to win it regularly. Here we're going to look through certain tips that will enable you to move into profitability.

Do Not Follow The Herd

This theory is also a basic yet misunderstood concept when it comes to capital market valuation issues. When it comes to precious trading insights and so-called insider reports, it's always quick to fall victim to the general flow of emotions. You want to move into the depths of it, and you will certainly be scared to lose out on what you see as the perfect opportunity to make money fast and effortless.

Banish Those Thoughts

We are simply coming at things from two slightly different angles, while not joining the group. In one, we don't encourage the simple seduction of stock tips by so-called experts to drag us and manipulate us. On the other side, we are not basing our own investment choices solely on what the general crowd is doing at the moment. At its heart, we will still depend on our own intuition, derived from the comprehensive fundamental and scientific modes of research, to process and make the requisite judgments about sales and transactions.

That's not to suggest we're not open to suggestions that might be coming from others. That surely is not true. Holding an open mind is important, the more from which to understand. My interpretation of this will be to interpret new ideas gleaned from others as just that - possible ideas. The filtration and analytical method that forms the foundation of the investment profession also need to be exposed to them. The ability to be caught away by the raw force of envy or terror in moments of intense emotion will be wonderful, so please try your utmost to stave it off. You're getting better off with it.

I've always found it simpler for me to avoid market calls during times of a bull run, as nearly any second person you encounter on the streets will be willing to talk on investments and give a bit of well-meaning sage guidance. I suppose a latent skeptic resides inside me, hoping for the smallest chance to pounce. Beyond the particular slant will be the foundation I have in the theoretical framework that I've come to depend on to make all of my investment decisions.

I realize that even though this proposed invitation to stock was to perform superbly well and my research did not lead me to take any decision for any reason or other, there will be some more concrete opportunities awaiting me. This eliminates the risk of losing out to basically none.

For circumstances when the stock market occurs, in those instances, it is typically uncertainty that is more prevalent. On many occasions, people will offer advice to keep out of the stock market or get out of stock until it gets too late. I find it more challenging to tackle fear than envy, which is natural. That's also part of why bear markets are always faster to set up than their bull equivalents. People get inspired by fear more quickly than by envy.

Also, the way to overcome this is to remain concentrated and firm in the critical process. I realize, for me, that every choice I make would be the product of philosophical and logical study, and that gives me the confidence to carry the choice through. This moves to the system's next step.

Trust Your System

You should feel at home because you value the mechanism, whether it's a down market or a bull market. This is because you have the trust and understanding that the method can produce a steady share of chances for you to step towards profitability.

However, one thing you can remember here is that you don't just pinch some old collection of technical indicators and then mark the framework. I tended to do so early on, and it was a common sight, so I bailed out of my investment choices, mostly at crucial junctures that might have had me earn gains rather than constant losses.

When I talk about the method, it's something I've built for myself. For me, I use a two-step method that requires the stock filtration to be done by the fundamental analysis, then the technical analysis to determine optimum entry and exit points. Some people are concerned with designing their structures solely on the basis of technological research, whilst some are only sticking to the basics. There is no solution that is correct or wrong. I guess the most practical way of looking at things will be which method will be deemed the best framework for you to achieve stable income over a fair period of time.

I notice that marrying the two major analytics schools fits pretty well for me because it offers me a sense of confidence that much of the angles should be guarded. When you're designing your ideal method, you have to determine what will best for you.

The theoretical part of business, including the statistical study of commodities, has its positives. Even they have their share of issues. No one method will ever assert outright dominance over the other, which is presumably why the one I use now always pulls elements from both.

You may notice that in designing your own ideal method, you have the same thoughts and perceptions as mine, and therefore build an amalgamation of the fundamental and the scientific. In other instances, you might be oriented more toward the scientific side of things, and the design might seem more like a graphical model. Whatever the case, the phase after the device is installed will be to thoroughly test it.

This is the position where you develop your faith.

Back checking is perhaps the most popular form people hire to verify a system's functionality and viability. For strictly technological tools, this approach is simple to apply since the test results can be collected within a matter of minutes these days. For the fundamentalists, back research is still feasible, but more manual of nature would have to be undertaken. In reference to the quarterly or annual accounts, they will have to review the change in market values. Back testing is useful for establishing a device base, but a separate type of testing is required to show it stressfully.

The use of the device in either simulated or live trading will be forward checking or experimenting in real-time. Such research will catch both the thoughts of the uncertain and the resulting reactions as the request is eventually proved to be right or incorrect. I carried on research with my method with approximately a year before raising the stakes on-investment decision.

The downside to forwarding testing is that it requires time, basically. This is not a workaround. The nice thing about that is that if you see it function regularly, you can develop a strong trust in the method. And if the device doesn't actually work, you will have learned useful experience of tinkering with it and coming up with more insights about how to make things better for you.

I will say you should actually get away with doing forward tests for only six months at this stage. I will suggest, when it comes to this subject, that the longer the time, the better. Of course, this has got to be matched with the question of what happens if the device simply doesn't function. This leads to the crucial issue of how you are formulating your method.

Take an individual who believes he would like to invest on the basis of leverage, for example. He provides an easy mechanism where, if his price reaches the 52-week high price watermark, he will go long or buy a warehouse. Since this is such an easy technique for him, he would be able to do back checking on this approach to verify its effectiveness. If he is pleased with the outcome of the back examination, he will then pass it on to the process of forwarding checking, where he will analyze the findings first hand. He would need to start worrying about the realistic implications of this technique, and during the live trading phase, he would have ample practice using it. He might care about choosing which stock to invest in when there could be several stocks in the same moment breaching their 52-week high watermark. He would also look at this methodology's total feasibility and make observations as to if it is worth following this course.

The method doesn't have to be very complex in general. It only needs to be important to you and, of course, potentially successful as utilized in the markets.

Market Timing

If you want to produce supernormal stock market returns, then I don't care what other people suggest, the timing of the market would be a talent you have to learn.

There will still be time to purchase inventories and time to market. A successful stock market company will require someone to take advantage of such two optimum timings and have the spirit to see beyond them.

Would you foresee returns to be reached if you only want to buy into a stock and keep it for posterity? Responding is true. You might, yes, but there will be better chances of having supernormal returns. There are also legends and legend investing that exist with individuals who have spent $5,000 and, after 30 years, have earned back a million dollars. All those reports will not be that these acquisitions were in the next major wave of businesses. It is almost about moving into Apple in early 2000 or some of the software giants.

It is not a daily thing that certain chances exist, and if skipped, it could very well be a wait that lasts for a lifetime to come. I put forward the notion of market timing to overcome this problem.

If you're willing to absorb the market's highs and troughs when it comes to business range, you don't need to really strike the jackpot.

Often, setting away the notion that you are going to purchase at the very lowest and offer at the very peak is fine too. Not a lot of people will do it. In reality, I haven't seen anybody at this stage of writing who can lay claim to regularly and conscientiously do it. We can consider reaching the seventy-fifth percentile level more frequently than not as a positive accomplishment. Selling the stock when it's a quarter of moving away from the very peak and purchasing the stock when it's a quarter of moving away from the very bottom, to me, are praiseworthy feats that will actually take several years of practice.

The other explanation that market timing is very important to producing the supernormal returns that one people expect in the equity market is the reality that the churning impact needs to be taken into account.

If, in the span of three years, a stock were to undergo a 100-point increase, it will be called quite a strong investment in most regions. Will it be possible if I were to suggest having five separate instances of 20 point increase within a year? First off, a 20 point increase will have a greater chance of occurring than a 100 point rise. Second, I'd only like to identify five separate places where there's a better chance of making a 20 point shift. It will also actually be better to notice five 20 point shifts in a year than to notice one 100 point step in one or two years. The argument I am suggesting is that with the timing of the business, you are able to generate a higher amount of profits over a greater range of transactions relative to getting all the earnings based on one or two firms.

Metaphorically, market timing will cause you to receive a dollar from any citizen on the globe, as opposed to earning ten dollars from everyone in your region. Will it be better to ask somebody to give you a dollar while you're worried about it, instead of asking them to part with ten dollars? The same goes for one warehouse. It would be a trifle tougher to bag a ten-bagger, as some Wall Street people would say it, due to having regular one bagger on yourself. One bag is equal to a fold increase of the purchase price for clarity purposes. This is one of the key reasons why I would suggest timing on demand to be one of the abilities that you will pick up while you advance in your investment career.

Here, nothing is completely crafted in stone or wood, as in many aspects in existence and in the markets too. Typically there are at least two sides of everything, and often even more than two. For this matter of market timing, amid my ongoing appeals for one to pick up this valuable talent, I do agree that for others, acquiring this ability may actually be pointless to them.

For certain people who are already guardians or husbanders with vast sums with assets and money, so I might sense that market timing skills would not be as important to them as they might be to the average retail investor. For these individuals born with incredibly significant quantities of wealth, they will genuinely carry out a buy and keep the policy that will continue for centuries. This is because their immediate needs are now well covered for the resources they have at their hands, and the immense surplus can be guided into savings that will practically bear fruit in a lifetime.

Not everybody is a scion of certain family riches or has the chance to accumulate a massive sum of money within a very short period. Quite a lot of people are already trying to keep the cash flowing in, and it's fairly much at the forefront of our heads as to how best to produce further gains on the money surplus.

Ultimately, utilizing market timing correctly and with proper implementation will then encourage one to speed up the compounding rate for one's capital.

Chapter 16: Glossary of terms

- Accounts Payable – a short term liability, representing money the company owes for purchases from a supplier

- Accounts Receivable – a short term asset, representing money the company is expecting to receive from sales made to customers

- Accrued Expenses – a liability, such as an obligation to pay interest to bank lenders or to pay taxes to the government

- Asset – a resource that the company owns or controls

- Book Value- The sum of all liabilities and equity on the balance sheet

- Balance Sheet – one of the three primary financial statements, which shows a snapshot of the assets, liabilities, and equity of the business at a certain point in time

- Brokerage Firm – A financial institution that facilitates the buying and selling of financial securities (generally stocks or bonds) between buyer and seller.

- Brand – A distinguishing symbol, mark, logo, name, word, sentence or a combination of these items that companies use to distinguish their product from others in the market. Brand equity is the positive sentiment created by a product among its target audience over time.

- Cash – the money a company has on hand, whether in physical currency or in bank accounts

- 12. Cash Flow – Cash flow or flows is the cash generated by a company. It is different from earnings because does not include non-cash items. For example, a company may make a large sale to a customer, which will count as earnings, but the customer has 30 days to pay for the purchase, so it is not yet cash received by the company.

- Creditors – Investors or institutions (such as banks, among others) to which a company owes money.

- Capital – Another word for money.

- Common Stock – the stock sold to investors on the market

- Cost of Goods Sold – the costs required to produce the good or service sold to a customer.

- Dividend – The portion of a company's profits that it pays out each year to shareholders in the form of cash.

- Discount Price- A price that is lower than the true value

- Discounted Cash Flow (DCF) Analysis- Forecasting future cash flows that the business will generate and then discounting them back to the present value at an appropriate discount rate.

- Discount rate- Rate of return that investors need to receive in order to be compensated for risk

- Diversification – A risk management technique that mixes a wide variety of investments within the portfolio. The rationale behind this technique contends that a portfolio of different investments will, on average, yield higher returns and pose lower risk than any individual investment found within the portfolio.

- Equity Value- Intrinsic value of equity that is found by subtracting total debt from firm value

- Enterprise or Firm Value – The total value of the company, including the portion of it that "belongs" to its creditors. It is calculated by adding the company's net debt to its market cap.

- Equity - the total of all stock owned and earnings retained that belong to the owners

- Economic Moat - The competitive advantage that one company has over other companies in the same industry. This term was coined by renowned investor Warren Buffett.

- Economic Moat - The competitive advantage that one company has over other companies in the same industry. This term was coined by renowned investor Warren Buffett.

- Equity Portfolio or Stock Portfolio - A basket or collection of stocks. A diversified stock portfolio includes companies from different industries and of different sizes.

- Firm/Enterprise Value- Intrinsic value of a company taking into account both debt and equity

- Gross Margin – the total revenue (or sales) minus the cost of goods sold

- Income Statement – one of the three primary financial statements, which shows the activity of a company over a period of time, showing both revenues and expenses

- Intrinsic Value – The true worth of a company. There are many ways to estimate the intrinsic value of a company, among them are discounted cash flow analysis and relative valuation analysis.

- Inventories – products that will eventually be sold to a customer

- Interest Coverage - The total value of the company, including the portion of it that "belongs" to its creditors. It is calculated by adding the company's net debt to its market cap.

- Investment Thesis - The basic guiding principles an investor establishes to justify:

    - Why he owns the company

    - What he expects to happen

    - What he sees that the market does not give the company credit for

- Liability - any obligation that the company owes to another entity 40). Long-term Debt - a liability such as a loan from a bank

- Liquidity - The degree to which an asset or security (stock) can be bought or sold in the market without affecting the asset's price or stock price. Assets that can be easily bought or sold are known as liquid assets.

- Low Cost Advantage – A sustainable advantage driven by access to a unique process, location, scale, labor costs or access to a unique asset, which allows a company to offer goods or services at a lower cost than competitors.

- Margin of Safety – Only purchase stocks when the market price is significantly below the intrinsic value. For example, a company owns land, equipment, cash and other assets that are worth $20 per share, yet the stock price is trading at $15 per share in the market. Buying this company at $15 provides a 25% discount or margin of safety.

- Mutual Fund – Professionally managed stock portfolio. Instead of investing in individual stocks yourself, you can invest money in a mutual fund, where professionals pick stocks for you.

- Market Value- the sum of the market cap (shares outstanding times total shares) and the debt

- Market Share – the percentage of a certain industry or market (e.g. the athletic shoe market) that a certain company's sales are

- Margins – The percentage of profit the company makes for every dollar of revenues. For example, a 50% profit margin means the company earns $0.5 of profit for every $1 of revenue earned.

- Market Capitalization (also known as market cap) – Total market value of the company's equity. It is calculated by multiplying the stock price of the company times the number of shares outstanding.

- Network Effect – A phenomenon whereby a good or service becomes more valuable when more people use it.

- Net Debt – The company's total debt adjusted by its cash on hand (total debt minus cash).

- Operating Expenses – the costs associated with operating the business, such as payroll, sales commissions, marketing, transportation, travel, and rent expenses

- Operating Income – the income after subtracting both cost of goods sold and operating expenses from total revenuesOperating Margin – calculated by dividing operating income by total revenues

- Operating Margin (EBIT Margin) – The profit the company makes after paying for its cost of goods sold and the cost of salaries, utilities, and depreciation.

(Operating Profit / Total Revenues)

- Profit Margins - The ratio of profits made per dollar of revenue. The higher the profit margin the better.

- Portfolio Manager - The manager of a portfolio of stocks. They do extensive research to make investment decisions for a fund or group of funds under their control. Based on their research, the Portfolio Manager will buy and sell stocks.

- P/E Ratio - One measure of how expensive a stock is. In general, a high P/E suggests that investors are expecting higher earnings growth to be high in the future. A low P/E can indicate either that a company may currently be undervalued or that the company's profits are expected to decline.

The price-earnings ratio can be calculated as: Market Value per Share (Stock Price) / Earnings per Share or Market Capitalization / Profits

- Property, Plant, & Equipment – the long-term physical assets owned by a company, including land, buildings, furnishings, and machinery

- Price to Book – A ratio used to compare a stock's market value to its book value. It is calculated by dividing the current closing price of the stock by the latest quarter's book value per share.

- Profits – Profit is the money a business makes after accounting for all the expenses. Regardless of whether the business is a couple of kids running a lemonade stand or a publicly traded multinational company, consistently earning profit is every company's goal.

Net Profits = Total Revenue – Total Expenses

- Retained Earnings – income generated by the business that has been reinvested in the business, rather than distributed to owners in a dividend

- Revenue – The amount of money that a company actually receives during a specific period. It is referred to as the "top line" because it is the total amount of sales before you start to factor in the costs of the business.

- Revenue (or Sales) – the total amount generated by sales to customers

- Return on Invested Capital – A calculation used to assess a company's efficiency at allocating capital under its control to profitable investments.

- Return on Capital – Return on Capital is a useful metric for comparing profitability across companies based on the amount of capital they use.

- Return on Equity (ROE) – Perhaps the most useful financial metric or all, it is used to compare a company's profits based on the total capital. Return on Equity = Net Income / Shareholder's Equity

Return on Equity = Net Income / Shareholder's Equity

- Statement of Cash Flows – one of the three primary financial statements, which shows all the sources and uses of cash over a period of time

- Stock – Stock is a unit of ownership in a company. When you buy a stock you become a shareholder, which means you own part of the company.

- Stock Market – The market in which shares of publicly-held companies are issued and traded, either through exchanges or over-the-counter markets. Also known as the equity market, it provides companies with access to capital (money) in exchange for giving investors a slice of ownership in a company.

- Shareholder – Any person, company, or other institution that owns at least one share of a company's stock. Shareholders are a company's owners.

- Stock Ticker or Symbol – An identifier (usually from 1 to 4 letters for US companies) for a stock. This symbol is the name under which a company's stock trades in the stock market.

- SWOT Analysis – A comprehensive analysis of a company's Strengths, Weaknesses, Opportunities and Threats.

- Shorting a stock – Borrowing against the shares of stock, you profit when the stock price goes down.

- Switching Costs – The inconveniences that dissuade a customer from switching to a competitor. The negative costs that a consumer incurs as a result of changing suppliers, brands or products. Although most prevalent switching costs are monetary in nature, there are also psychological, effort and time-based switching costs.

- Ticker – The abbreviation that a company is listed on the stock exchange. For example, Google has the ticker GOOG and Apple has the ticker AAPL.

- Valuations – A way to gauge how expensive a stock is. Commonly used methods are the price of the share relative to earnings per share (P/E Ratio) and the price per share relative to the book value per share (P/ Book ratio). The higher the valuations, the more growth you need to justify the investment.

Conclusion

The market is only a market, no feeling and no connection attach to it. There's nothing exciting about this, nor is it particularly thrilling. For others, the major problem is that they choose to mess up the investment market with capital, or, more accurately, assets that they expect to buy.

Please step away from the pedestal, and turn aside from your feelings.

The more dispassionate and comparatively calm you are willing to keep with respect to capital market activities and machinations or any asset sector, the easier that will be with your overall investment effort.

To me, the best approach of this book will still be to go back to the fundamentals for the experienced traveler or for the novice. Have a clear idea of what type of business you're working with. For starters, if you plan to restrict your search to just the S&P 500 index stocks, then research such stocks and come to understand the behavior of the index like you might change your own body.

This, of course, may not happen immediately, and to strive for it will take regular, diligent action.

The next move will be to devise the hunting plan or hunting method with the clearness of the goals. This is where hundreds of people will be gunning for the simple way out, seduced by this or that ready-made machine offered by glib salespeople who pledge for a commitment of only one hour a day to roll in riches.

Little is really good for free. Only think of the duck swimming serenely on the lake's shore, when in reality, it is actively paddling to stay afloat under the waters. This can also be a harbinger about how the particular structure builds.

You can run into dead ends, and in anger, you can start pulling the hair out of its roots. That is completely natural. What counts most here will be the tenacious endeavor to build your own workable method. I can just advise you- don't give up. Eventually, you would be able to locate the framework because when you believe it and start seeing the steady benefits from it, even the struggles they followed, it would make their effort worth it.

It's my sincere wish that you might produce steady gains from the investment market, and who knows, maybe one day you'd be able to leave your day job and live to live entirely off the stock market income.

Never give up.

Made in the USA
Coppell, TX
02 March 2021

51157997R00216